OBAMA: YEAR ONE

Thomas R. Dye
Florida State University

George C. Edwards III
Texas A&M University

Morris P. Fiorina
Stanford University

Edward S. Greenberg
University of Colorado, Boulder

Paul C. Light
New York University

David B. Magleby
Brigham Young University

Martin P. Wattenberg
University of California, Irvine

Longman

New York   San Francisco   Boston

London   Toronto   Sydney   Tokyo   Singapore   Madrid

Mexico City   Munich   Paris   Cape Town   Hong Kong   Montreal

Editor-in-Chief: Eric Stano
Marketing Manager: Lindsey Prudhomme
Associate Development Editor: Donna Garnier
Project Coordination, Text Design, and Page Makeup: Grapevine Publishing
    Services, Inc.
Copyeditor: Leslie Ballard
Cover Designer/Manager: Wendy Ann Fredericks
Cover Photo: © Callie Shell/Aurora
Manufacturing Buyer: Roy Pickering
Printer and Binder: Courier-Stoughton
Cover Printer: Courier-Stoughton

Obama: Year One, by Thomas R. Dye et al.

1 2 3 4 5 6 7 8 9 10–CRS–12 11 10 09

Longman
is an imprint of

ISBN 13: 978-0-205-79822-3
ISBN 10:   0-205-79822-5

www.pearsonhighered.com

TABLE OF CONTENTS

Author Biographies..v

Chapter One: Culture War? The Road To and From 2008.........................1
   Morris P. Fiorina, *Wendt Professor of Political Science,*
      Stanford University

Chapter Two: How Barack Obama Changed Presidential Campaigns...........31
   David B. Magleby, *Dean of the College of Family, Home and Social*
      Sciences, Brigham Young University

Chapter Three: The Presidential Media Environment in the Age of Obama.....55
   Martin P. Wattenberg, *Professor of Political Science,*
      University of California, Irvine

Chapter Four: Obama and the Federal Bureaucracy..................................73
   Paul C. Light, *Paulette Goddard Professor of Public Service,*
      New York University

Chapter Five: Government and the Economy...85
   Edward S. Greenberg, *Director of the Political and Economic Change*
      Program, University of Colorado, Boulder

Chapter Six: A Full Plate: The Obama Policy Agenda...............................91
   Thomas R. Dye, *Emeritus McKenzie Professor of Government,*
      Florida State University

Chapter Seven: *Creating* Opportunities for Policy Change?.....................103
   George C. Edwards III, *Distinguished Professor of Political Science,*
      Texas A&M University

AUTHOR BIOGRAPHIES

Thomas R. Dye, Emeritus McKenzie Professor of Government at Florida State University, regularly taught large introductory classes in American politics. He received his B.A. and M.A. degrees from Pennsylvania State University and his Ph.D. degree from the University of Pennsylvania. He is the author of numerous books and articles on American government and public policy, including *Politics in America; The Irony of Democracy; Politics in States and Communities; Understanding Public Policy; Who's Running America; American Politics in the Media Age; Power in Society; Politics, Economics, and the Public*, and *American Federalism: Competition Among Governments*. His books have been translated into many languages, including Russian and Chinese, and published abroad. Dye has served as president of the Southern Political Science Association, president of the Policy Studies Organization, and secretary of the American Political Science Association. He has taught at the University of Pennsylvania, the University of Wisconsin, and the University of Georgia, and served as a visiting scholar at Bar-Ilan University, Israel; the Brookings Institution in Washington, D.C.; and elsewhere. He is a member of Phi Beta Kappa, Omicron Delta Kappa, and Phi Kappa Phi and is listed in most major biographic directories. Additional information is available at www.thomasrdye.com

George C. Edwards III is Distinguished Professor of Political Science at Texas A&M University. He also holds the George and Julia Blucher Jordan Chair in Presidential Studies and has served as the Olin Professor of American Government at Oxford and the John Adams Fellow at the University of London, and has held senior visiting appointments at Sciences Po-Paris, Peking University, Hebrew University of Jerusalem, and the U.S. Military Academy at West Point. A leading scholar of the presidency, he has authored dozens of articles and has written or edited 23 books on American politics and public policy making. He is also editor of *Presidential Studies Quarterly* and general editor of the *Oxford Handbook of American Politics* series. His latest book, *The Strategic President*, offers a new formulation for understanding presidential leadership.

Professor Edwards has served as president of the Presidency Research Section of the American Political Science Association, which has named its annual dissertation prize in his honor and awarded him its Career Service

Award. A member of Phi Beta Kappa and a Woodrow Wilson Fellow, he has received the Pi Sigma Alpha Prize and the Department of Defense's Decoration for Distinguished Civilian Service. He is also a member of the Council on Foreign Relations. He has spoken to more than 200 universities and other groups in the U.S. and abroad, keynoted numerous national and international conferences, done hundreds of interviews with the national and international press, and can be heard on National Public Radio. Dr. Edwards also applies his scholarship to practical issues of governing, including advising Brazil on its constitution and the operation of its presidency, Russia on building a democratic national party system, Mexico on elections, and Chinese scholars on democracy. He also authored studies for the 1988 and 2000 U.S. presidential transitions.

Morris P. Fiorina is Wendt Professor of Political Science and Senior Fellow of the Hoover Institution at Stanford University. He received a B.A. from Allegheny College in Meadville, Pennsylvania, and a Ph.D. from the University of Rochester. Before moving to Stanford, he taught at the California Institute of Technology and at Harvard University.

Fiorina has written widely on American government and politics with special emphasis on representation and elections. His books include *Representatives, Roll Calls, and Constituencies*; *Congress—Keystone of the Washington Establishment*; *Retrospective Voting in American National Elections*; *The Personal Vote: Constituency Service and Electoral Independence* (coauthored with Bruce Cain and John Ferejohn); *Divided Government*; *Culture War? The Myth of A Polarized America* (coauthored with Samuel Abrams and Jeremy Pope), and the forthcoming *Disconnect: The Breakdown of Representation in the United States* (with Samuel Abrams). He has served on the editorial boards of a dozen journals in the fields of political science, economics, law, and public policy, and from 1986 to 1990 he served as chairman of the Board of Overseers of the American National Election Studies. He is a member of the National Academy of Sciences.

In his leisure time, Fiorina favors physical activities, including hiking, fishing, and sports. Although his own athletic career never amounted to much, he has been a successful youth baseball coach for fifteen years. Among his most cherished honors is a plaque given by happy parents on the occasion of an undefeated Babe Ruth season.

Edward S. Greenberg is a research program director in the Institute of Behavioral Science at the University of Colorado, Boulder and professor of political science. He received his B.A. in chemistry from Miami University and his Ph.D. in political science from the University of Wisconsin. Before joining the UC faculty, he held political science faculty appointments at Stanford University and Indiana University.

Ed Greenberg's research and teaching interests include American government and politics, domestic and global political economy, and democratic theory and practice, with a special emphasis on workplace issues. He is the author or coauthor of several books including *The Struggle for Democracy*, 9th edition (Pearson Longman, 2009, with Ben Page), *America's Democratic Republic*, 3rd edition (also with Ben Page), *The American Political System*, 5th edition (1989), *Workplace Democracy* (1986), *Capitalism and the American Political Ideal* (1985), and *Serving the Few* (1974). Ed Greenberg has been the recipient of three major grants from the National Science Foundation and two from the National Institutes of Health, totaling more than $2.5 million. His book (with Leon Grunberg, Sarah Moore, and Pat Sikora) *Turbulence: Boeing and the State of American Workers and Managers* will be published in Spring 2010 by the Yale University Press.

Although he enthusiastically takes part in all officially sanctioned and socially acceptable Boulder, Colorado leisure activities—hiking, biking, and skiing—Ed is happiest hanging out and reading in sidewalk cafes and coffee-houses and sampling the fare in the city's many fine restaurants with his wife Martha. He also is inordinately proud of his two sons, who, in addition to their many accomplishments, have shown the good sense to live in cities Ed and Martha love to visit: San Francisco and Seattle.

Paul C. Light is the Paulette Goddard Professor of Public Service at New York University's Wagner School of Public Service. He received his B.A. from Macalester College and his Ph.D from the University of Michigan. Professor Light has a wide-ranging career in both academia and government. He has worked on Capitol Hill as a senior committee staffer in the U.S. Senate and as an American Political Science Association Congressional Fellow in the U.S. House. He has taught at the University of Virginia, University of Pennsylvania, and Harvard University's John F. Kennedy School of Government. He has also served as a senior adviser to several national commissions on federal, state, and local public service. He is the author of 15 books on government, public service, and public policy. Light's current research focuses on government reform, Congress, the presidency, and social entrepreneurship. His latest books are *A Government Ill Executed* (Harvard University Press, 2008) and *The Search for Social Entrepreneurship* (Brookings Institution Press, 2008). He was the founding director of the Brookings Institution's Center for Public Service and continues his research on how to invite Americans to serve their communities through public service. His work has been funded by the Douglas Dillon Foundation, the Pew Charitable Trusts, the David and Lucille Packard Foundation, among many others. He is also an expert on preparing government, charitable organizations, and private corporations for natural and human-made disasters, and was a recognized leader in the response to Hurricane Katrina in 2005. He has testified before Congress more than a dozen times in the last five years.

David B. Magleby is nationally recognized for his expertise on direct democracy, voting behavior, and campaign finance. He received his B.A. from the University of Utah and his Ph.D. from the University of California, Berkeley. Currently Distinguished Professor of Political Science, Senior Research Fellow at the Center for the Study of Elections and Democracy, and Dean of the College of Family, Home and Social Sciences at Brigham Young University, Professor Magleby has also taught at the University of California, Santa Cruz, and the University of Virginia. He and his students have conducted statewide polls in Virginia and Utah. For the 1998–2008 elections he has directed national studies of campaign finance and campaign communications in competitive federal election environments involving a consortium of academics from nearly 80 universities and colleges in 38 states. This research is summarized in six edited books. In addition, he is co-editor of a longstanding series of books on financing federal elections. In partnership with colleagues, he has been studying the implementation of new voting technology, work funded in part by the National Science Foundation. He has been a Fulbright Scholar at Oxford University and a past president of Pi Sigma Alpha, the national political science honor society. Magleby is the recipient of many teaching awards including the 1990 Utah Professor of the Year award from the Council for the Advancement and Support of Education and the Carnegie Foundation, the 2001 Rowman & Littlefield Award for Innovative Teaching in Political Science, and several department and university awards. At BYU he served as Chair of the Political Science Department before being named dean. He is married to Linda Waters Magleby. They are the parents of four and grandparents of one.

Martin P. Wattenberg is professor of political science at the University of California, Irvine. His first regular paying job was with the Washington Redskins, from which he moved on to receive a Ph.D. at the University of Michigan. He is the author of *Is Voting for Young People?*, which is part of Longman's "Great Questions in Politics" series. In addition, he is the author of several books published by Harvard University Press: *Where Have All the Voters Gone?* (2002), *The Decline of American Political Parties* (1998), and *The Rise of Candidate-Centered Politics* (1991).

Professor Wattenberg has lectured about American politics on all of the inhabited continents. His travels have led him to become interested in electoral politics around the world. He has co-edited two books published by Oxford University Press—one on party systems in the advanced industrialized world, and the other on the recent trend toward mixed-member electoral systems.

Chapter 1

Culture War?
The Road To and From 2008

Morris P. Fiorina

In November of 1989 the Berlin Wall came down. In October of 1990 Germany was reunified. On Christmas Day 1991 the Soviet Union ceased to exist. After observing these rapid history-changing developments, political scientist Sidney Verba quipped that "before the collapse of the Soviet Union, no one would have predicted it; afterwards everyone could explain why it was inevitable."[1]

Political developments in the United States between 2005 and 2008 do not compare in historical significance with the collapse of the Soviet Union and the end of the Cold War. But they have in common the feature that the 2008 outcome was completely unanticipated by politicians and politicos only a few years earlier. To close observers, political status quos sometimes appear firmly grounded and durable when they are, in fact, unstable and fragile. The events of 2005 to 2008 suggest that this was the case for the status quo of the Clinton–Bush years, a status quo with roots in the events and social changes of the 1960s, and one that seemed disconnected from the broader public, and unresponsive to its concerns. Although few could have foreseen it in the aftermath of the Republican victory in 2004, that election now appears to have been the last hurrah of the electoral order that began to take form in the 1960s and reached fruition with the election of Ronald Reagan in 1980.[2] This chapter develops these arguments and provides some supporting evidence.

THE SECOND TERM OF GEORGE W. BUSH

Within six months of the 2004 election, President Bush's approval ratings slipped below 50 percent (Figure 1). During the next four years his ratings continued to drop, interrupted by only periodic small recoveries. By the time the 2008 elections took place, the president's approval ratings were flirting with historical lows—and his *disapproval* ratings set a new historical high mark.[3]

Figure 1. Gallup Approval Rating of George W. Bush

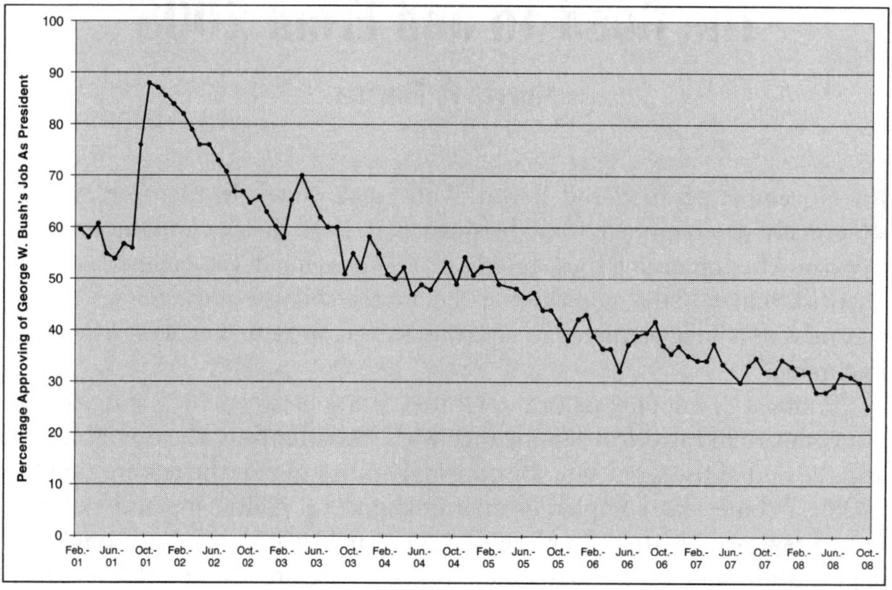

Source: The Gallup Organization.

Some analysts pinpoint the Bush administration's much-criticized response to the devastation of New Orleans by Hurricane Katrina in September of 2005 as the beginning of the administration's political end. But as Figure 1 shows, the president's fortunes had begun to slip well before Katrina. By all accounts, both the electoral and legislative strategies of the administration had focused on winning by minimal majorities. The upside of such a strategy is obvious: Fewer compromises will be necessary if fewer people need to be persuaded or bought. The downside is equally obvious: There is less of a margin for error in the event of miscalculations or adverse developments, of which there were both.

Shortly after his reelection, the president announced that he would spend some of his political capital on an ambitious reform of the Social Security system, including the creation of private accounts. This was not an issue he had emphasized in the campaign and one that quickly proved a nonstarter. By summer, congressional Republicans had quietly buried the proposal. In early August 2005 President Bush signed a pork-stuffed transportation bill that contained more than 6,000 congressional earmarks, about 40 times as many as were contained in a bill Ronald Reagan vetoed in 1987 (although that bill was passed by a Democratic Congress), further irritating economic conservatives already upset by the administration's borrow-and-spend proclivities. A month after Katrina the president nominated his longtime aide and confidante, Harriet Miers, to the Supreme Court. Miers had somewhat less than stellar qualifications, sparking a palace revolt in establishment conservative circles that resulted in Bush withdrawing the nomination less than a month later.

By early 2006 some nervous Congressional Republicans were beginning to put distance between themselves and the administration. Congressional opposition scuttled the administration's plan to lease six U.S. ports to a company owned by Dubai in the United Arab Emirates. A few Republicans began to speak out against the conduct of the war in Iraq, where violence associated with the insurgency increased through 2006. By summer it was apparent that a good Democratic year was in the offing. President Bush's approval ratings were stuck in the 35- to 40-percent range, and by the time Congress adjourned and the campaign began in earnest, majorities of Americans had come to believe that the Iraq War had been a mistake and had not made America safer. Some polls even showed that the public now judged Democrats equally as capable of dealing with the terrorist threat as Republicans—Homeland Security, the Republican trump card in the two preceding elections—no longer gave them an edge.

Virtually everyone expected the Republicans to lose seats in both chambers of Congress, although not so many that they would lose control of either chamber. But as time went on, expected losses mounted. Outside the South, where the president remained popular, Republican candidates began to separate themselves from him, requesting that he not campaign for them, and highlighting areas of disagreement to demonstrate their independence. (A few candidates declined to appear with the president when he visited their states.) Some conservative commentators published essays contending that the party deserved to lose.[4] A majority of the American public apparently agreed with this sentiment. In the November voting, the Republicans suffered a stunning defeat as the Democrats defeated six incumbent Republican senators to take control of the Senate by a razor-thin 51–49 majority, and gained 30 seats in the House of Representatives to take control of that chamber by a more comfortable margin.

The 2006 elections showed that the vote divisions apparent in the 2000–2002–2004 election period were less fixed than many Republican operatives and political commentators had assumed. The exit polls indicated that Democrats and Republicans voted much the same in 2006 as in 2004—self-identified Democrats were about four percent more Democratic in their voting and self-identified Republicans about two percent less Republican, but independents were 17 percentage points less Republican. The decisions of American voters were more contingent than many campaigners and commentators believed.

The election postmortems abandoned the red–blue polarization narrative that had dominated the previous decade of electoral commentary. Instead, the 2006 election was "the revenge of the center," "the revenge of the independents," "a move back to the political center," the result of "a rising radical center," and an indication that both parties had better "heed voters' call for moderation."[5] A new consensus held that the elections had "buried the notion that swing voters are a dying breed and that elections are won by mobilizing the base."[6]

After poking through the electoral carnage, the media collectively decided that the once-brilliant election strategy followed by Karl Rove, Bush's chief adviser, was not so brilliant after all. The elections had dashed Rove's dream of emulating William McKinley and building a Republican majority that would govern for the next generation.[7] (Adding insult to injury, Newt Gingrich, the architect of the 1994 Republican revolution, denounced Rove's campaign strategy of relying on the base as "maniacally dumb.")[8] Even members of the Republican general staff expressed second thoughts. Former Republican National Chair Ken Mehlman cautioned, "We have to win back the confidence we lost in '06 from swing voters and ticket-splitters."[9] And pollster Matthew Dowd criticized President Bush for following the advice he had given the president in 2004: "I think we should design campaigns that appeal not to 51 percent of the people, but bring the country together as a whole."[10]

After the 2006 election, some Republicans consoled themselves with the expectation that their congressional losses would be reversed in 2008. Indeed, the historical record shows that big losses in one election often are followed by big gains in the next one. In 1964, for example, the Republican lost 57 House seats in the Lyndon Johnson landslide, but promptly won 47 seats back in the 1966 midterm election. The difference in 2007–2008, however, was that the unfavorable conditions that generated the 2006 Republican losses did not improve; on the contrary, they worsened. The president's approval ratings continued to decline, and while the "surge" reduced the violence in Iraq, polls indicated that the public had grown tired of the continued American commitment and its cost in money and blood. Then came the economic meltdown. What started as a supposedly "contained" problem with subprime mortgages metastasized into a full-blown stock market crash in September of 2008, and what now looks to be the most serious recession in at least several decades.

THE 2008 CAMPAIGN

Given developments in 2006 and 2007, it was clear that the political winds would be behind the 2008 Democratic presidential nominee. Indeed, political science statistical models that predict election outcomes based on the "fundamentals" of the economy and peace and war forecast a comfortable Democratic victory—if prevailing conditions failed to improve.[11] Half a dozen serious contenders entered the field, but the odds-on favorite for the Democratic nomination was Senator Hillary Clinton of New York. Although some establishment Democratic leaders feared that she would be too polarizing a nominee, she was the wife and partner of the only victorious Democratic presidential candidate since 1976 (and the only one reelected since Franklin Roosevelt), she enjoyed near-universal name recognition, and with the vaunted Clinton machine at her disposal and a wide lead in the early polls, Clinton began the Democratic contest in a strong position.

The story on the Republican side was much less clear. An early favorite was Senator George Allen of Virginia, a southerner who was broadly acceptable to the various factions of the Republican Party. But Allen suffered defeat in his 2006 bid for re-election to the Senate after a series of revelations involving ethnically insensitive remarks, Confederate flags, and unusual intrafamily conflicts, leaving the Republican field wide open.

Republicans had numerous choices, half a dozen of them reasonably serious, but all faced opposition from various factions of the party. Probably, former Tennessee senator and professional actor Fred Thompson had the greatest potential to unify the party, but he appeared to be an unenthusiastic candidate and his campaign never caught fire. "America's mayor," former New York City Mayor Rudy Giuliani, appealed to national security and foreign policy hard-liners, but his liberal positions on abortion, gay rights and gun control made him unacceptable to social conservatives. The folksy former governor of Arkansas, Mike Huckabee, appealed to social conservatives, but economic conservatives were unenthusiastic about his populist-leaning economic positions. Former Massachusetts Governor Mitt Romney appealed to business conservatives, but social conservatives suspected his midnight conversion to pro-life and antigay marriage positions (his membership in the Mormon Church was an additional negative for some.) Libertarians unhappy with Bush administration policies on the war, government spending, civil liberties and social issues found a champion in Representative Ron Paul of Texas. No particular faction liked Arizona Senator John McCain, and some conservative notables such as Rush Limbaugh and Ann Coulter strongly opposed him, but he won anyway.[12] Like many journalists and political scientists, we regarded first Giuliani, then later McCain as the strongest Republican candidates, in large part because of their potential to draw support from independent and moderate voters in a race against Hillary Clinton, widely viewed as a partisan Democrat despite her moves to establish a more centrist image while in the Senate.

By late 2007 hints of electoral change were in the air. Social conservative leaders briefly discussed the possibility of launching a pro-life third-party candidacy when Giuliani established a strong lead in early polls. Faced with the likely prospect of a race between Hillary Clinton and a conservative Republican, Unity08, an Internet bipartisan movement, raised the possibility of drafting Democrat (but former Republican) New York Mayor Michael Bloomberg, or some other centrist alternative candidate, a prospect reportedly considered by Bloomberg himself. As the primary season approached, commentators began to speculate that the Democratic nomination would be decided quickly—Clinton would wrap it up on Super Tuesday, while the Republican nomination contest might go all the way to the convention. But in early February Obama defeated Clinton in the Iowa caucuses and prevailing expectations were roundly upset. For a brief period we even fantasized about a Giuliani v. Obama contest that would thoroughly scramble the voting alignments of 2000 and 2004.

The Obama campaign has been and will continue to be a fascinating subject for journalists and politicos.[13] For our purposes, the essential fact is that a candidate of a younger generation—and a member of a racial minority group, at that—was able to defeat Clinton running on a very unspecific platform of "change." Nonincumbent candidates typically promise change, of course, but Obama emphasized his desire to transcend the bitter partisanship and stale politics that prevailed in Washington. He promised to adopt a more civil, inclusive governing style, and to search for common ground in an attack on the country's problems. Pragmatism, not ideology, was the watchword. None of this is to overlook the importance of his early opposition to the war in Iraq, his superbly organized campaign, his exploitation of new technology, or the strategic and tactical mistakes made by the Clinton campaign, but only to emphasize the message that animated the Obama campaign, a message that promised a break with the politics of the past several elections.

While Clinton had greater appeal to some elements of the traditional Democratic coalition such as blue-collar workers, senior citizens (especially older women), minority group members other than African Americans, and self-identified Democrats, Obama appealed more to the young, African Americans, the well-educated, and people who viewed themselves as independents. Notably, Obama was endorsed by prominent red state Democrats who believed that his broader appeal would enable him to run better in their states, and thus help candidates further down the ticket, than would a Democrat like Clinton with a more partisan image.[14]

The 2008 elections demonstrated that the contingency shown by voters in 2006 was not a one-shot occurrence. Turnout typically rises about 50 percent from the midterm to the presidential election, and the lion's share of that increase comes from the ranks of the independents and weaker partisans who are less motivated to vote in the midterm elections. That held true in the 2008 elections as turnout rose to about 62 percent and political independents and ideological moderates continued to move to the Democrats, resulting in Republican defeats even in states and districts not thought vulnerable a year before the election. Nine states that had been Republican red in 2004 went into the blue Democratic column in 2008, and after losing eight more Senate seats and another 21 House seats the Republican presence in Congress was reduced to the levels that prevailed prior to the 1994 "Republican Revolution."

THE ELECTORATE IN 2008

In addition to holding political positions that are more polarized than those held by the general public, members of the political class differ from the public in two other important ways. First, their priorities differ—they often are motivated by issues to which the general public assigns relatively low priority. Second, holding positions that are more extreme and feeling more intensely about their issues, members of the political class often adopt a more conflictual, uncivil style in communicating their views.[15]

The prime example is the cluster of social issues widely viewed as the basis of the so-called culture war. There is more common ground on such issues than is usually recognized, and Sunshine Hillygus and Todd Shields reported that the public attached low priority to such issues even in 2004, an election some journalists and politicos erroneously interpreted as determined by "values" issues like abortion and gay marriage.[16] Numerous polls in recent years continue to document the marginal status of social issues in the larger public. One standard question format lists a series of current issues and asks voters how important each issue will be when they decide how to vote in the upcoming election. Table 1 reports such a poll conducted by the Pew Research Center as the congressional campaigns began to get underway in the summer of 2006. Of the 19 issues included in the survey, immigration occupied the position of median importance (despite a major battle that had taken place in Congress the previous month). The issues above the median were those of broad importance to Americans' everyday lives—their jobs and their children's educations, their health care and social security, and, of course, terrorism and the war in Iraq. The issues below the median included many of those that take up so much space and time in our media. Abortion and gay marriage came in dead last. The public actually viewed flag burning as more important than gay marriage. The Democratic political class should not take unalloyed satisfaction in polls like this—the public also attached relatively little importance to government surveillance and global warming.

Table 1. Importance of Issue for Voting in 2006.

	(Percent of Registered Voters)	
	Very %	Not at all %
Education	82	3
Economy	80	1
Health Care	79	1
Social Security	75	1
Situation in Iraq	74	2
Terrorism	74	2
Taxes	68	2
Job Situation	66	4
Energy Policy	64	2
Immigration (Median)	58	5
Budget Deficit	56	4
Environment	52	3
Minimum Wage	52	8
Flag Burning	49	22
Government Surveillance	44	11
Inheritance Tax	44	13
Global Warming	44	11
Abortion	43	15
Gay Marriage	34	33

Source: June 2006 Pew Poll. http://people-press.org/reports/questionnaires/279.pdf#search=%22June%202006%22

Table 2 reports the results of a similar poll conducted for CNN in the summer of 2008 (well before the meltdown in the fall turned the media's klieg lights on the economy). The results are similar to those in 2006. Taxes occupied the position of median importance. The same broad issues as in 2006 lie above the median, while social issues like gay–lesbian rights, gun control, and abortion bring up the rear. Again, Democratic leaders might be surprised to see that the public regards race relations as relatively unimportant, perhaps a reflection of Obama's nomination.

Table 2. Importance of Issue for Voting in 2008.

	(Percent of Registered Voters)	
	Extremely/Very %	Not at all %
Economy	93	1
Iraq	84	3
Health Care	83	3
Education	83	3
Terrorism	77	4
Gas Prices	77	5
SS/Medicare	77	4
Taxes (Median)	74	5
Illegal Immigration	67	9
Environment	66	7
Foreign Trade	65	7
Gun Policy	53	19
Abortion	50	25
Race Relations	48	23
Gay-Lesbian Issues	36	37

Source: CNN/Opinion Research Corporation Poll. June 26–29, 2008.
N=906 registered voters.

Beyond the immediate sting of the losses suffered in 2008, at least four features of the voting point to serious problems for Republican prospects in future elections.

1. Latinos

The exit polls indicate that the inroads into the Latino vote made by George W. Bush in 2004 were lost in 2008: The vote for Barack Obama was 8 to 13 percentage points higher than for John Kerry.[17] The Hispanic vote probably contributed to McCain's loss of several western states. Given that the number of Hispanic Americans now exceeds the number of African Americans, and that their numbers are projected to grow, the electoral importance of this constituency will only increase over the next few election cycles. But the presence of strong anti-immigration and nativist sentiments in the Republican base poses a serious obstacle to winning votes among what other Republicans view as a culturally conservative, economically entrepreneurial constituency that should be susceptible to Republican appeals.

Immigration is not a simple issue. Surveys show that Americans clearly differentiate between legal and illegal immigration, but a majority opposes the "enforcement only" policy advocated by many in the Republican base, and favors a policy along the lines of the "enforcement plus path to citizenship" legislation advocated by the Bush administration but rejected by the Republican Congress.[18] There are some tensions within the Democratic Party between those ideologically favorable to ethnic minorities and those more pragmatically concerned about the impact of immigrant labor on low-wage workers. In addition, some state and local Democratic officials in severely impacted states like Arizona and New Mexico have taken strong stands against illegal immigration. But, on the whole, the divisions within the Republican Party are much deeper that those in the Democratic Party. Business conservatives see a need for low-wage immigrant labor, libertarians ideologically favor immigration, and pragmatists believe the party has no choice but to woo such an important constituency. Meanwhile, social conservatives and nativists oppose immigration, many quite vociferously. We see no easy compromise position for Republicans, so the party's difficulties with Latinos are likely to persist.

2. The Young

Another group that swung significantly against the Republicans in 2008 was young(er) voters. According to the exit polls, voters in the 18 to 29 age group voted 12 percentage points more for Obama than for Kerry, and voters in the 30 to 44 age group voted 6 percentage points more for Obama. Younger voters are not inherently more liberal than older voters—in the 1980s younger voters showed more movement toward Ronald Reagan and the Republicans than did older voters—but young voters are less stable in their political behavior because their more limited political experience makes them more reflective of current political conditions and events (voters 45 and older voted only 2 percentage points more for Obama than for Kerry). Thus, younger voters are not permanently lost to the Republicans, but recapturing previous levels of support would require some combination of Democratic failure and Republican change.

Age is an ambiguous variable in political discussions specifically and social science research generally. In some cases it indicates different life stages with different concerns. For example, a person's attitudes toward taxes may change between the time they are a footloose and fancy-free 20-year-old, and the time that they are a married 50-year-old with a mortgage(s) and children in college. In other cases, age differences reflect different generational experiences that persist through a person's lifetime: an older generation's experience simply differs from a younger's. We believe that there are important generational factors at work in our current politics.

As noted by President Obama in *The Audacity of Hope*, much of contemporary American politics has roots in the social changes and controversies of the 1960s.[19] Indeed, when we look at the leadership cadres of the various cause groups associated with the parties, it is striking how old they are.[20] During the Democratic nomination contest some older feminists expressed disappointment that their younger sisters were not flocking to the side of Hillary Clinton, but were in many cases supporting an inexperienced younger male.[21] Feminist icon Gloria Steinem famously claimed in a *New York Times* op-ed that sexism was a more restrictive force in American politics than racism.[22] Ms. Steinem is now 75 years old. Betty Friedan, the intellectual mother of the modern feminist movement, died in 2006 at the age of 79. Eleanor Smeal, twice president of the National Organization for Women (NOW) and publisher of *Ms*. magazine, is now 70. Kate Michelmann, former longtime president of the National Abortion and Reproductive Rights Action League (NARAL) is now 66.

To a significant degree the religious right rose in reaction to the agenda of the modern feminist movement. Former presidential candidate and founder of the Christian Coalition of America, Pat Robertson, is now 79 years old. Louis Sheldon, founder of the Traditional Values Coalition, a leading antigay rights organization, is now 75. Jerry Falwell, founder of the Moral Majority, died in 2007 at the age of 73. James Dobson of Focus on the Family, currently the most important religious right organization, resigned as chair in early 2009 at the age of 73.

None of the above is meant as a criticism of senior citizens being politically active, but only to emphasize the age of many of the people who are most concerned with issues surrounding gender roles, the traditional family and sexual mores. And the point is not limited to these issues. More generally, we can cite similar statistics about aged leadership of the civil rights movement and the conservative movement.[23] The simple fact is that the agendas that have dominated American politics in recent decades are primarily the agendas of people who are getting quite long in the tooth.

Now consider the American electorate as it exists in 2009. More than a quarter of the voting age population—the so-called Millennial generation, has been born since 1976, two years after the resignation of Richard Nixon, which officially ended "the sixties."[24] For them, the sixties are like the Great Depression is to the baby boomers; they know it only secondhand from the tales told by parents and grandparents. Another 20 percent of the electorate, Generation X, was born between 1965 and 1976. If we make the reasonable assumption that little or nothing of current politics registers with people younger than eight or nine years old, most of these Americans have little more experience with the events of the sixties than the Millennials. Political leaders may be more comfortable fighting on familiar terrain, but that terrain is unfamiliar to nearly half of the potential electorate, and that fraction is only growing.

Both parties have aging leadership, of course, but the Democrats seem to have gotten the jump on rejuvenating their party, perhaps because of electoral losses in the 2000s. When Republicans attacked Obama as a socialist, even a Marxist, I wondered how many Americans today even understand the meaning of such terms, let alone react to them with any emotion? Certainly, I say very little about socialism and Marxism in the introductory political science course I teach. The Berlin Wall fell before today's freshmen were born, and the elections of Ronald Reagan and British Prime Minister Margaret Thatcher, which drove a stake through the hearts of avowedly socialist parties, were three decades ago. Whatever the short-term electoral necessities in 2008, John McCain's strategy of targeting older white voters in places like Appalachian Pennsylvania holds little long-term promise for Republicans.

3. Independents

The electoral and governing strategies of concentrating on the base were predicated on the belief that true independents had become so scarce that it no longer made sense to tailor party appeals for them.[25] Since this belief apparently conflicts with much popular commentary about the size of the independent bloc, some explanation is necessary.

From the New Deal of the 1930s to the Reagan era of the1980s, the Democrats enjoyed a significant edge over the Republicans in the partisan loyalties of the population. In the 1980s Republicans closed much of the gap. Between the end of the Reagan years and the 2004 elections Americans who self-identified as Democrats were on average a bit more than one-third of the eligible electorate, those who identified as Republicans a bit more than one-quarter, and independents made up the balance (Figure 2). But during this period some political scientists and politicos argued that a large proportion of independents—more than two-thirds—who conceded leaning toward a party were actually "closet partisans," so that true independents numbered in single digits as a proportion of the electorate.[26]

This is not the place to present a major argument, but I believe that treating leaning independents as partisans because they largely cast their presidential votes in the direction they lean, is problematic.[27] In the National Election Studies (NES) panel surveys the self-identification of leaners is less stable than that of self-identified weak partisans, and it seems just as plausible that independents base their answer to the question of their leanings on how they intend to vote as on the opposite supposition, thus reversing the commonly assumed causal link.

Figure 2. Partisan Self-Identification of the American Public

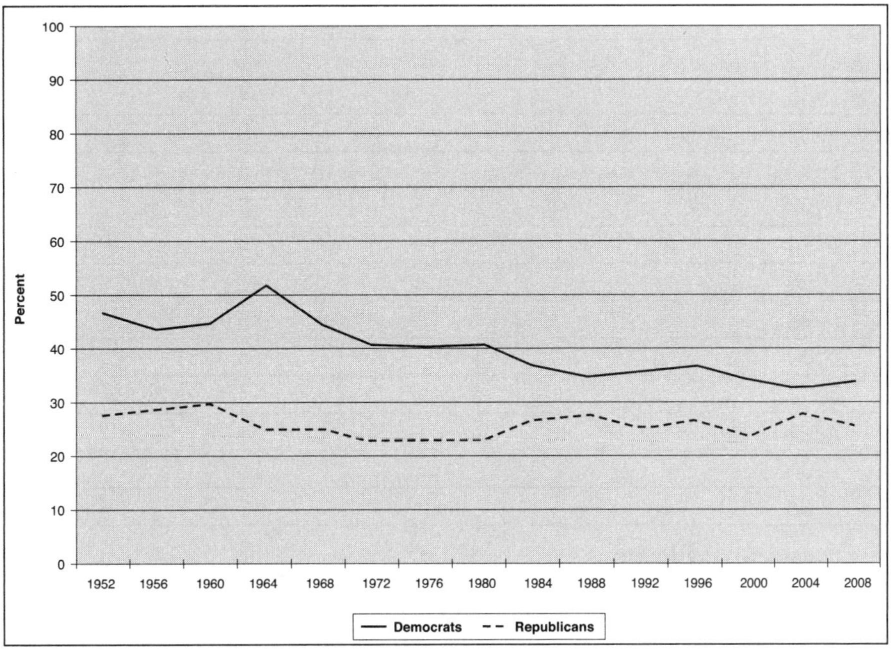

Source: The American National Election Studies

At any rate, much of the political change in the 2006–08 elections can be attributed to the actions of the supposedly endangered species of independents. There is nothing new here. The Republican takeover of Congress in 1994 was greatly aided by support from 1992 candidate Ross Perot voters, many of whose partisan affiliations were weak or nonexistent.[28] Self-identified independents voted for Republican congressional candidates over

Democrats that year by a margin of 14 percentage points. As shown in Table 3, in succeeding elections Republicans ran a very close race with Democrats among independents—until 2006, which saw a deficit of 18 percentage points. In the 2008 election the Republican deficit was only half as large as in 2006, but independents made up a larger share of the larger 2008 electorate (29 percent) than of the smaller 2006 electorate (26 percent).

Table 3. How Independents Vote (Exit Polls)

	% Republican – % Democrat
House Elections	
1976	-10
1980	+11
1982	-2
1984	+7
1986	-4
1988	-8
1990	-6
1992	-7
1994	+14
1996	+2
1998	+3
2000	+3
2002	+3
2004	-3
2006	-18
2008	-8
Presidential Elections	
1976	+4
1980	+25
1984	+28
1988	+14
1992	-6
1996	-7
2000	+2
2004	-2
2008	-8

Source: National Exit Polls, Roper Archive.

In the presidential voting, the importance of independents is even clearer. Between 1952 and 2004 the Republicans won 9 of 14 elections while never having as many partisan adherents as the Democrats. Independents largely made up the Republican partisan deficit. Since the coming of reliable survey data, George W. Bush in 2004 was the first Republican presidential winner who lost the independent vote. Although he squeaked by, his negative margin in 2004 quadrupled for McCain in 2008, who did not.

The good news for the Republican Party is precisely that independents tend to be swing voters.[29] In principle, recapturing a larger share of the independent vote does not present as serious a problem as capturing a larger share of the Latino vote, for if independents turned sharply Democratic in recent elections because they disapproved of the policies and performance of the Bush administration, they will listen to Republican appeals again if the Obama administration fails to perform or pushes unattractive policies. The bad news for the Republican Party is that, as discussed below, much of its leadership believes that the path to political revival depends on purging moderates and reemphasizing the purity of the party. In general, purer means smaller.[30]

4. Partisan Change

Independents are not the only partisan category that is a concern for Republicans. As Figure 2 suggests, there is also a problem with Republicans— that is, *former* Republicans—as well. The decline in Republican identification apparent in the 2008 NES survey is relatively small, but virtually every commercial poll reported a decline in Republican identification relative to Democratic between 2004 and 2008, many of them larger than that shown in the NES. Some polls showed more movement away from the Republican than toward the Democratic Party and others the opposite, but there is little doubt that after the 2008 election fewer Americans considered themselves Republicans than did after the 2004 elections.[31]

The nature of party identification continues to be an unsettled subject in political science. One school of thought (the traditionalists) believes that it is much like a religious identification in that it forms before issue preferences and ideological positions and, once formed, it changes only under the most extreme circumstances (Civil War, Great Depression).[32] Others (the revisionists) believe that while "sticky," party identification reflects and changes with current issues and government performance.[33] The relative decline in Republican identification between the 2004 and 2008 elections shown in the polls is consistent with the revisionist view.[34] In recent presidential elections partisans have tended to vote consistently with the way they label themselves close to 90 percent of the time. So the drop-off in Republican identification is potentially serious. If it just reflects a one-time disillusionment with the performance and policies of the George W. Bush administration, the long-term damage may not be serious.[35] But especially if the policies and performance of the Obama administration meet with widespread approval, the Republicans could be facing a long-term electoral disadvantage like they faced in the mid-20th century, although as yet, not nearly as large. (Recall, however, that although the Republican partisan deficit reached its maximum after the 1964 elections, the winner of the next presidential election was a Republican.)

A TRANSFORMATIVE ELECTION?

After every election the winners and losers contest its meaning. In general, the winners over-interpret the significance of the outcome and the losers under-interpret it. So it was in 2008. After the election some Republicans contended that the Obama victory was unimpressive. Looked at from the long historical standpoint since 1828 when direct popular voting began to determine the outcome, the Obama margin of the two-party vote was 26th of 47 margins—below the median (Table 4). But this comparison includes numerous instances of incumbents winning reelection or one candidate of the incumbent party succeeding another (e.g., FDR, Harry Truman). A more appropriate comparison is "party replacement elections," when the candidate of an "out" party defeats the candidate of the incumbent presidential party. As Table 5 shows, there have been 15 such elections since the replacement of the congressional caucus system by popular voting. Obama's 2008 margin falls just above the median. Moreover, several of the larger margins are misleading. In 1860 Lincoln won only 40 percent of the popular vote in a four-way race, and in 1912 Wilson won only 42 percent when the Republican Party split between former President Theodore Roosevelt and incumbent President William Howard Taft. In 1932, Franklin Delano Roosevelt (FDR) won during the greatest economic crisis in American history. In more normal times, only Eisenhower in 1952 and Reagan in 1980 won by somewhat bigger margins than Obama, although Reagan failed to bring in a Republican House of Representatives. The historical record shows that Americans rarely change parties in huge numbers, as in 1920 or 1932. Thus, it seems fair to conclude that the 2008 Democratic victory is pretty respectable, especially when coupled with the congressional gains in 2006.

But is it in popular jargon, a "transformative," election, or in the terminology of academic political science, a "realigning" election?[36] While many Democrats hope that is the case, and some—especially on the left of the Democratic Party—claim that is the case, such a conclusion would be at the least premature.[37] Elections, even landslide elections, are not transformative in themselves. Rather, significant electoral victories provide opportunities for the victors to transform the electoral landscape.[38] Sometimes the public approves of the victors' actions and the result is a new electoral order, as with Roosevelt in the 1930s and Reagan in the 1980s. At other times a major electoral victory appears to be only a historical interruption rather than a new era (e.g., 1952), or it even may be a precursor of major electoral trouble to come (e.g., 1964).

Table 4. Presidential Election Margin of Victory

Presidential Election Winner	Election Year	Margin of Victory
Harding (R)	1920	26.2%
Coolidge (R)	1924	25.2
Roosevelt (D)	1936	24.3
Nixon (R)	1972	23.2
Johnson (D)	1964	22.6
Roosevelt (R)	1904	18.8
Reagan (R)	1984	18.2
Roosevelt (D)	1932	17.8
Hoover (R)	1928	17.4
Jackson (D)	1832	16.8
Ike (R)	1956	15.4
Wilson (D)	1912	14.4
Van Buren (D)	1836	14.2
Jackson (D-R)	1828	12.4
Buchanan (D)	1856	12.2
Grant (R)	1872	11.8
Ike (R)	1952	10.7
Lincoln (R)	1860	10.4
Lincoln (R)	1864	10.2
Roosevelt (D)	1940	9.9
Reagan (R)	1980	9.7
Taft (R)	1908	8.6
Clinton (D)	1996	8.5
Bush (R)	1988	7.8
Roosevelt (D)	1944	7.5
Barack Obama	2008	7.2

Source: The Federal Election Commission.

Table 5. Party Replacement Election Margins

1920 Harding (R)	26.2%
1932 F. Roosevelt (D)	17.8
1912 Wilson (D)	14.4
1952 Eisenhower (R)	10.7
1860 Lincoln (R)	10.4
1980 Reagan (R)	9.7
2008 Obama (D)	7.2
1852 Pierce (D)	6.9
1840 Harrison (D)	6.1
1992 Clinton (D)	5.6
1896 McKinley (R)	5.3
1848 Taylor (R)	4.8
1892 Cleveland (D)	3.0
1844 Polk (D)	1.4
1884 Cleveland (D)	.7
1888 Harrison (R)	–.8

As critics point out, the realignment paradigm was overly idealized in scholarly writing of the 1960s to 1980s.[39] And David Brady has shown that some generally recognized realignments (those of the 1860s and 1890s) took place with relatively small electoral shifts—much smaller than the massive voting changes of the 1930s that are sometimes taken as the typical case of realignment. What appears to be necessary is for a new majority, even a small one, to win full control of the government and govern in a way that is satisfactory to a majority of the electorate.[40]

In that light, whether 2008 is transformative in the way that some now claim will all depend on the actions of the Obama administration and the effects of those actions, plus events and developments over which the administration has little or no control. Seldom has a president taken office under such inauspicious conditions: two wars, international terrorism, a major worldwide recession, and a looming entitlement crisis a little farther in the future.[41] The upside, of course, is that the bar has been set pretty low. Franklin Roosevelt and the New Deal Democrats did not work any miracles in the 1930s, but compared to what had gone before, voters at the time evidently felt that they were doing well enough.

WHITHER REPUBLICANS?

In the aftermath of the 2008 elections, some Republicans simply shrugged and pointed to the data in Figure 1. What would you expect to happen to candidates who shared the party label of a historically unpopular president in a time of economic difficulty and ongoing war? This sentiment is consistent with the view of many political scientists. As noted above, predictive models based on the "fundamentals" of economic and international conditions generally predicted a Democratic victory. And while detailed political science research on the 2008 elections is not available at the time of this writing, preliminary reports indicate that the election played out about as expected by the models.[42] To Republicans who accept this line of thinking, the Republican "brand" needs no major reformation. The United States is still a center-right country, voters' bad memories of the Bush administration will gradually fade, the Democrats will over-reach and under-perform, and the status quo of the early 2000s will be restored.

Other Republican commentators saw the election outcome as a reflection of more serious underlying problems, and vigorous arguments in the electronic and print media ensued. One common line of argument asserted that the Republican Party had strayed from fundamental principles. According to conservative columnist Deroy Murdock, "The GOP has been laid low, thanks to politicians who swapped their principles for power and lost both." As for "Comrade George W. Bush, . . . as a delivery system for socialism, he has been the most effective Trojan Horse since that pine steed rolled into Troy." And Republican congressional leaders share the blame for supporting the president ". . . amid an atmosphere of corruption, incompetence, and unaccountability."[43] Well, if that is the diagnosis, then the treatment is clear: "excommunicate the heretics."

But who are the heretics? Here the disagreement begins. While everyone can agree that corruption and incompetence are violations of basic principles of ethics and good management, what about policy positions that are sincerely held? Among the various factions of the Republican Party the disagreement can be as great as between the Democratic and Republican mainstreams. On the question of the war in Iraq in particular and the nation-building enterprise in general, so-called "paleoconservatives," like Pat Buchanan, have been almost as severe and unrelenting in their criticism as liberal Democratic denizens of the netroots.[44] Paleoconservatives favor a clear "America first" policy which supports international intervention only when critical national interests are threatened.[45] And economic nationalism should reign in economic policy. With their protectionist economic positions and nativist cultural positions the paleos have a populist tinge. They deride so-called "national greatness conservatives" like David Brooks and William Kristol as "borrow and spend conservatives" and "big government Republicans."

Also called neoconservatives, national greatness conservatives are anti-antigovernment.[46] That is, they argue that the traditional antigovernment mantra of conservatives is an inadequate governing philosophy. Abraham Lincoln and Theodore Roosevelt are Republican heroes who actively expanded national power and prestige. As for specific policies, just as Roosevelt attacked the private monopolies of his time, so conservatives today should attack public monopolies in education, health, and Social Security. An activist government in the domestic sphere is not necessarily bad, but conservative principles such as individual responsibility should inform government programs. After 9/11, neoconservatives supported an interventionist foreign policy that actively sought to spread democracy to other countries.

Libertarians disagree with the neoconservatives in the realm of foreign affairs: The undeclared war in Iraq is unconstitutional, and contrary to neoconservative thinking, nation-building is not the job of the U.S. government—even if the government were competent to do it. Libertarians generally condemn what they view as violations of civil liberties under the Bush administration. They oppose government bailouts of private industries and corporations, whereas paleos see a bailout of the auto industry as a matter of keeping manufacturing jobs in the United States.[47] In contrast to the "culture of life" philosophy of the paleos and social conservatives, many libertarians are pro-choice and favor gay marriage (or removing marriage from the hands of the state altogether). And, of course, while Pat Buchanan rails against illegal immigration, the libertarian-leaning *Wall Street Journal* editorial page advocates a liberal immigration policy.

Many Republicans believe that too-close adherence to socially conservative policy positions has hurt the party among independents, moderates, and the young. After the election, conservative humorist P. J. O'Rourke wrote in a serious vein, "If the citizenry insists that abortion remain legal—and, in a passive and conflicted way, the citizenry seems to be doing so—then give the issue a rest."[48] Former New Jersey Governor Christine Todd Whitman warns that "unless the Republican Party ends its self-imposed captivity to social fundamentalists, it will spend a long time in the political wilderness."[49] Kathleen Parker, a conservative columnist, provoked a flurry of Internet commentary when she wrote that ". . . the evangelical, right-wing, oogedy-boogedy branch of the GOP is what ails the conservative party and will continue to afflict and marginalize its constituents if reckoning doesn't soon cometh."[50] Conservative professor Jeffrey Hart agrees: "The lethal problem for Republicans is that while religion of a particular kind is central to their party today, it is also toxic to moderate, independent, suburban, young and, more inclusively, educated voters."[51]

Not surprisingly, social conservatives strongly disagree. Rod Dreher retorts that "To scapegoat religious conservatives for the recent Republican Party's implosion is preposterous."[52] He asks, "Was it the religious right that conceived and executed the disastrous Iraq War? Did preachers deregulate Wall Street? Did evangelical leader James Dobson screw up [FEMA's] response to Hurricane Katrina? Jack Abramoff—did he concoct his crooked lobbying schemes during long protest vigils outside abortion clinics?"

Similarly, Ross Douthat asks, "And why should abortion opponents, of all conservative factions, take the blame for the financial meltdown, or the bungled occupation of Iraq, or the handling of Hurricane Katrina?"[53] Ramesh Ponnuru flatly rejects any notion that the Republican Party should deemphasize social issues: "About this campaign to sideline the social Right, three things can be said with a fairly high degree of confidence: It is predictable; it will fail; and it is wrong."[54]

In perhaps the most original argument for Republican rebranding, Ross Douthat and Reihan Salam argue that Republicans should become the party of Sam's Club.[55] They argue that the old image of the party as the country club party is badly outdated. Rather, the most reliable Republican voters now come from the working and lower-middle classes. These Americans are not traditional small government conservatives; their views reflect their exposure to today's increasingly uncertain and rapidly changing cultural and economic environments. The Republican Party should transform its appeals to solidify its support among such voters. This would mean policies that provide income security (even wage subsidies in the case of the working poor), family friendly programs, health care, and tax reforms. Much of this sounds suspiciously like Democratic Party concerns, but Douthat and Salam argue that new programs should be devised to make maximum use of traditional conservative principles like personal choice and individual responsibility, and with careful attention to incentives. Conservative columnist Michael Barone retorts that such a strategy would tie Republican fortunes to a declining demographic and urges going upscale instead.[56]

As this brief survey suggests, there appears to be no majority position among the various Republican factions. Indeed, it seems to us that the modal position favors the ejection of some other faction of the party, usually moderates, although there is not universal agreement about what constitutes a moderate. Sometimes it is defined in policy terms—anyone not holding an absolutist position on some particular issue, and sometimes as a matter of style—anyone willing to compromise on some particular issue.

As disinterested observers, it appears to us that Republicans today are indeed in a difficult position. We think that the data support the conclusion of nonpartisan elections analyst Charlie Cook that "Those who write off the 2008 election by saying that Republican candidates weren't conservative enough are in denial. They are political ostriches, refusing to acknowledge that the country and the electorate are changing and that old recipes don't work anymore."[57] Consider the claim that the United States is a center-right country. That claim appears to reflect data such as that depicted in Figure 3. Whether one examines surveys from the NES, the General Social Survey (GSS), or Gallup, the ideological self-identifications of the American public follow a consistent pattern. The modal category is moderate/middle-of-the-road, followed closely by conservative, and more distantly, by liberal. If one combines the moderates and conservatives, there is a 75 percent center-right majority.

Figure 3. Ideological Self-Identification of the American Public

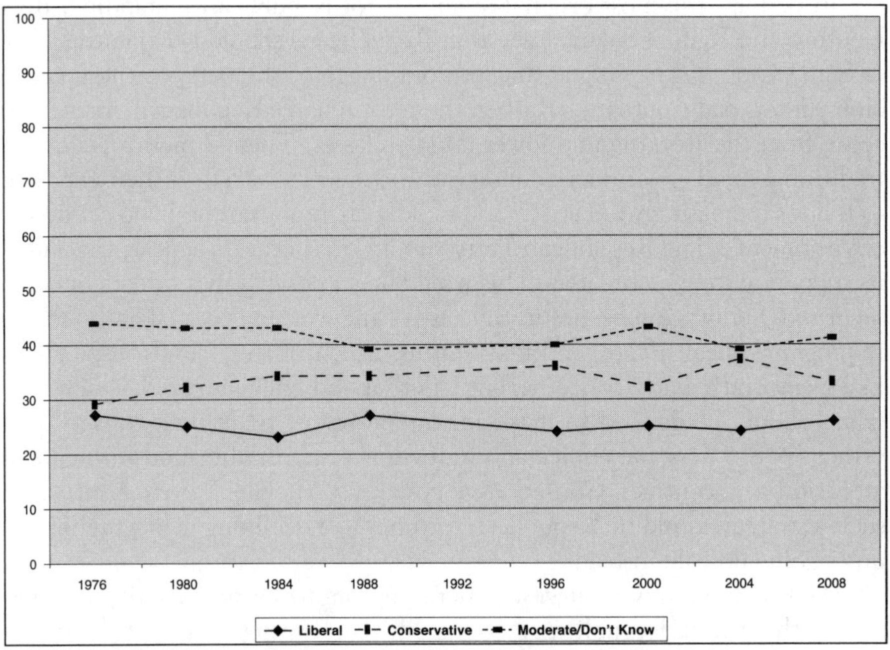

Source: General Social Survey. Data does not exist for 1992.

Note: Original 7-Pt Scale. Recoded: Liberal = Slightly Liberal, Liberal, and Extremely Liberal; Moderate/Don't Know = Moderates and Don't Knows; Conservative = Slightly Conservative, Conservative and Extremely Conservative.

But there are at least two qualifications to this conclusion. The first is that no law of nature dictates that moderates have to combine with conservatives. If moderates join with liberals instead, there is a 65 percent center-left majority—not as big, but still quite large. And the farther that Republicans move to the right on any issue cluster, the greater the likelihood that moderates will find themselves closer to liberals than to conservatives on such issues.

A second problem is that adopting the conservative label conveys less information about policy positions than ideologues and politicos might think. Four decades ago, Lloyd Free and Hadley Cantril reported that Americans appeared to be philosophically conservative and operationally liberal in that they preferred the conservative label to the liberal label, but simultaneously favored liberal policies over conservative policies.[58] That disparity persists according to recent research by Christopher Ellis and James Stimson.[59] Looking at the social welfare and moral/cultural policy positions held by self-identified liberals and conservatives in the 2000 NES, Ellis and Stimson report that people who adopted the liberal label espoused liberal policy positions much more consistently than people who adopted the conservative label espoused conservative policy positions. Nearly two-thirds of liberals favored liberal social welfare policies and liberal moral policies and another 20 percent were New Deal liberals—liberal on social welfare but conservative on moral issues. Self-identified conservatives in contrast, were far less consistent. Only one-quarter were conservative on both social welfare and cultural issues. The largest category—about a third—were cultural conservatives but not economic conservatives, and about a tenth were libertarians—culturally liberal and economically conservative. One of five self-identified conservatives was not conservative on *either* issue cluster. Data like these throw considerable light on the rejection of President Bush's proposal to add private accounts to Social Security.[60] Looking at the proportion of Americans who adopt the conservative label would lead to a serious overestimation of the proportion that would support such a policy change.

As for the tensions between social, economic, and neoconservatives, and the unattractiveness of the first's platform to critical groups of swing voters, it appears that Republicans are between a rock and a hard place. There is little or no possibility of following the advice of Whitman, Parker, Hart and others quoted above. In the first place, as suggested by the Ellis and Stimson findings, social conservatives are the single most numerous faction in today's (reduced in size) Republican Party. Informal reports indicate that they control a majority of the state parties. Thus, they are more capable of expelling other factions than vice versa. And what would be the result if they could be expelled? According to one blogger, what would be left "is the party of all the remaining Episcopalians, Californians and New Yorkers who prefer lower taxes."[61] It probably wouldn't be as bad as all that, but there is little reason to believe that a split with social conservatives would improve Republican electoral prospects in the short run.

The long run may be the problem, however. The positions and priorities of social conservative leaders today are at odds with those of younger Americans, moderates, independents, and suburbanites, who find themselves closer to Democrats on moral and cultural issues. Republican candidates like Rudy Giuliani and Arnold Schwarzenegger (and Mitt Romney in his Massachusetts days) could put even seemingly dark blue states into play, but in most states social conservatives block the nomination of such potentially competitive candidates.[62] A continued emphasis on abortion, gay and lesbian issues, stem cell research, assisted suicide, and other "culture of life" issues may assure a solid, but losing—and declining—share of the national vote.

Of course, change is constant. It is possible that public opinion could shift toward the views of social conservatives. Or the Obama administration could fail so abysmally that a Republican victory is assured despite its positions on cultural and moral issues (remember the Democrats' electoral nosedive between 1964 and 1968). Perhaps the most likely—if least recognized—possibility is change among social conservatives themselves. Even the evangelical base within the social conservative faction is not as homogeneous in political views as claimed either by their leaders or their liberal opponents; they are not all carbon copies of James Dobson and Louis Sheldon. Nearly one-quarter of white evangelicals voted for Obama in 2008, and their views on culture of life issues are more heterogeneous than most observers would assume. Furthermore, as noted above, much of the present social conservative leadership is aging. There is considerable recent commentary on generational change occurring within the evangelical movement.[63] Younger leaders continue to hold conservative positions on the so-called "below the belt" issues, but have expanded their agenda to include concerns such as environmental stewardship, third world poverty, and other issues on which their positions are closer to the positions and priorities of groups that are more distant on the traditional issues of abortion and gay/lesbian rights. Even on abortion and gay/lesbian issues, there is some talk within evangelical circles of deemphasizing legal and legislative strategies in favor of changing hearts and minds through the agencies of civil society.[64] In the long run, leadership responds to changing conditions. Ideologues and dogmatists who refuse to change lose influence within their own organizations and are pushed aside by more pragmatic challengers, or their organizations themselves decline and are replaced by others better adapted to new conditions.[65] It is unlikely that what is written about social conservatives in 2016 will be the same as what was written about them in 2004–2008.

A FINAL THOUGHT

We are reasonably confident that the old political order born with Ronald Reagan's election and evolving through the 2000s has come to an end. We have no confidence in our ability to predict the shape of the new order that is now being birthed. Consider that the New Deal Democratic coalition splintered in the mid-1960s, but the shape of the new order did not emerge until Reagan's election more than 12 years later. One might object that a new Republican order had emerged immediately but that it was short-circuited by the impeachment and resignation of Richard Nixon. The counter-objection is that there was a clear distinction between the international and domestic policies of the Nixon and Reagan administrations; Reagan did not simply pick up the interrupted agenda of Nixon. Moreover, consider that after Reagan's victory in 1980, it took the Democrats another 12 years before Bill Clinton hauled the party back into competitive territory. All of this is simply to say that the country could be in for an extended period of political uncertainty, and the Republicans could be in for a long sojourn in the electoral wilderness.

For now, it matters little what Republicans do or say. The ball is in the Democrats' court. On the one hand they take full control of the national government under terribly difficult circumstances. But the challenges the country faces are a political opportunity. If the Obama administration meets with considerable success, political historians may look back and judge that 2008 indeed was a transformative election. But the downside is that with full control of the national government comes full blame for failure. If the administration fails in the eyes of the public, there will be no place for Democrats to run or hide.[66] If, as seems most likely at the time of this writing, the public judges the administration's performance as somewhere in between, then uncertainty reigns. From survey evidence it appears that Obama has moved farther in the direction of interventionist government than many moderate voters are comfortable with. But if the Republicans fail to reinvent their party quickly enough, the results could be a more left-of-center government than a majority would like, just as the Bush years saw a more right-of-center government than a majority would have liked. Americans can only choose between the alternatives offered by the parties.

QUESTIONS TO CONSIDER

1. Some argue that the Republican Party's old image of the "country club party" is badly outdated, and the party should rebrand, becoming the party of Sam's Club. What does "rebranding" mean? How do you think the party should rebrand, or what else do you think should be the party's focus?
2. The nature of party identification is controversial in political science. Two schools of thought are discussed in this chapter—the traditionalists and the revisionists. Describe and compare their basic beliefs. Which do you favor and why?
3. In determining if a presidential election is a "transformative" election or a "realigning" election, what factors are considered?

NOTES

[1]Sydney Verba, personal conversation.

[2]Just as the Democratic landslide of 1964 appears to have been the last hurrah of the New Deal electoral order, although that was not clear until the 1980s. On the concept of an electoral order see Byron E. Shafer, "The Notion of An Electoral Order: The Structure of Electoral Politics at the Accession of George Bush," in *The End of Realignment? Interpreting American Electoral Eras*, ed. Byron E. Shafer (Madison: University of Wisconsin Press, 1991), pp. 37–84.

[3]Gary Jacobson, "Congress: The Second Democratic Wave," *The Elections of 2000*, ed. Michael Nelson (Washington, DC: CQ Press, 2010), p. 100.

[4]For example, Cait Murphy, "Why the Republicans Need to Lose," *CNN Money.com*, October 25, 2006. http://money.cnn.com/2006/10/23/news/economy/pluggedin_murphy_election.fortune/index.htm (accessed October 29, 2009).

[5]Quotations from E.J. Dionne Jr., "Democrats Won with Votes on Loan," *realclearpolitics.com*, http://www.realclearpolitics.com/, November 9, 2006. Chuck Todd, "Congress Gets a Case of the Blues," *nationaljournal.com*, http://www.nationaljournal.com/njonline/, November 8, 2006. David Ignatius, "A Move Back to the Political Center?" *realclearpolitics.com*, October 18, 2006. E.J. Dionne Jr., "Rising Radical Center," *washingtonpost.com*, http://www.washingtonpost.com/, October 24, 2006: A19. Mort Kondracke, "Democrats, GOP Should Heed Voters' Call for Moderation," *realclearpolitics.com*, January 4, 2007.

[6]Craig Charney, "Why Dems Won," *nypost.com*, http://www.nypost.com//, November 10, 2006.

[7]Jacob Weisberg, "Karl Rove's Dying Dream," *nypost.com*, http://www.nypost.com//, November 2, 2005.

[8]Quoted in Jim Rutenberg, "Gingrich Lambastes President and Rove, nytimes.com, May 30, 2007.

[9]Jim VandeHei, Mike Allen, and Jonathan Martin, "Republicans Fear 2008 Meltdown," *The Politico*, http://www.politico.com/, May 29, 2007.

[10]Jim Rutenberg, "Ex-Aide Says He's Lost Faith in Bush," *The New York Times*, April 1, 2007. http://www.nytimes.com/2007/04/01/washington/01adviser.html (accessed October 29, 2009). According to reporter Thomas Edsall, analyses by Dowd had convinced Rove to abandon the "compassionate conservative" approach of 2000 in favor of the base strategy of 2004. Thomas Edsall, *Building Red America* (New York: Basic, 2006), pp. 50–52.

[11]James E. Campbell, ed., "Forecasting the 2008 National Elections," *PS: Political Science & Politics* 41(2008), pp. 679–732.

[12]Greater appeal to independents enabled McCain to win several crucial open primaries, that is, primaries where independents could vote. Exit polls indicated that Mitt Romney would have won New Hampshire and Mike Huckabee South Carolina if only self-identified Republicans had been permitted to vote. This was a matter of some irritation to Republicans like Coulter and Limbaugh.

[13]For example, Brian Stelter, "The Facebooker Who Friended Obama," New York Times, July 7, 2008. John Heilemann, "The New Politics: Barack Obama, Party of One," New York Magazine, January 11, 2009. "Obama Campaign head gets big book Deal," AP, February 4, 2009, http://www.msnbc.msn.com/id/29012117/ (accessed October 29, 2009).

[14]Governor Kathleen Sebelius of Kansas and Senator Claire McCaskill of Missouri are two prominent examples. In addition, House Speaker and Convention Chair Nancy Pelosi's thinly disguised support for Obama was attributed in part to the belief that he would be of more electoral help to House candidates running in Republican regions than would Clinton.

[15]These arguments are developed more fully in Morris P. Fiorina, with Samuel J. Abrams, Disconnect: The Breakdown of Representation in American Politics (Norman, OK: Univ of Oklahoma press, 2009), Chap. 3.

[16]D. Sunshine Hillygus and Todd Shields, "Moral Issues and Voter Decision Making in the 2004 Presidential Election," PS:Political Science & Politics 38(2005), pp. 2001–08.

[17]The imprecision of the estimate reflects controversy over the level of Hispanic voting for Bush in 2004. See David L. Leal, Matt A. Barreto, Jongho Lee, and Rodolfo O. de la Garza, "The Latino Vote in the 2004 Election," PS: Political Science & Politics 38 (2005), pp. 41–49. All 2008 election poll data cited in this chapter are as reported on the CNN Web site, http://www.cnn.com/ELECTION/2008/results/polls/#USP00p1 (accessed October 29, 2009).

[18]For a discussion of the complexity of public opinion on immigration see Morris P. Fiorina, et. al.,"The Immigration Issue," The New American Democracy (New York: Longman, 6th ed., 2009), pp. 116–119.

[19](New York: Crown Publishers, 2006), pp. 29–42.

[20]For a more extensive discussion see Fiorina and Abrams, Disconnect: The Breakdown of Representation.

[21]For replies to such reproaches from their elders see Betsy Reed, "Race to the Bottom," The Nation, May 19, 2008, http://www.thenation.com/doc/20080519/betsyreed (accessed October 29, 2009). Caille Millner, "When Can I Call Myself a Feminist Again?," San Francisco Chronicle, May 5, 2008.

[22]Gloria Steinem, "Women are Never Front-Runners," New York Times, January 8, 2008.

[23]Fiorina and Abrams, Disconnect: The Breakdown of Representation, chap. 8.

[24]Note to younger readers: In pop culture as well as social science, the "60s" encompasses the period extending from the assassination of President Kennedy in November of 1963 to the resignation of President Nixon in August of 1974.

[25]For a fuller discussion of the logic of the base strategy, see Fiorina and Abrams, Disconnect: The Breakdown of Representation, chap. 8.

[26]The strongest statement to this effect is Bruce E. Keith, David B. Magleby, Candice J. Nelson, Elizabeth Orr, Mark C. Westlye, and Raymond E. Wolfinger, The Myth of the Independent Voter (Berkeley: University of California Press, 1992).

[27]Warren Miller, "Party Identification, Realignment, and Party Voting: Back to Basics," American Political Science Review 85(1991), pp. 557–68.

[28]On the views of Perot voters see Paul R. Abramson, John H. Aldrich, and David W. Rohde, Change and Continuity in the 1992 Elections (Washington, DC: CQ Press, 1994), pp. 192–93.

[29]Mayer reports that in the 1972–2004 elections inclusive, 40 percent of pure independents were swing voters, compared to 27 percent of independent leaners, 28 percent of weak parti-

sans, and only 12 percent of strong partisans. William G. Mayer, "What Exactly is a Swing Voter? Definition and Measurement," *The Swing Voter in American Politics*, ed. William G. Mayer (Washington, DC: Brookings, 2008), p. 11.

[30]A case in point: Shortly after this chapter was written, Pennsylvania Senator Arlen Specter switched from the Republican Party to the Democrats after deciding that he could not win the 2010 Republican primary in a state where self-identified Republicans had become less numerous, and, as a consequence, probably more conservative since 2004.

[31]For data and discussion see David W. Brady, Douglas Rivers, and Laurel Harbridge, "The 2008 Democratic Shift," *Policy Review* 152 (2008–09), pp. 3–13.

[32]Angus Campbell, Philip E. Converse, Warren E. Miller, and Donald E. Stokes, *The American Voter* (New York: Wiley, 1960), chap. 7. Donald Green, Bradley Palmquist, and Eric Schickler, *Partisan Hearts and Minds* (New Haven, CT: Yale, 2002), chap. 2.

[33]John E. Jackson, "Issues, Party Choice, and Presidential Votes," *American Journal of Political Science* 19(1975), pp. 161–85. Morris P. Fiorina, "An Outline for a Model of Party Choice," *American Journal of Political Science* 21(1977), pp. 601–25. Benjamin Page and Calvin Jones, "Reciprocal Effects of Party Preferences, Party Loyalties, and the Vote," *American Political Science Review* 73 (1979), pp. 1071–89.

[34]If the change were entirely due to an influx of new voters who disproportionately identified as Democrats, that would be consistent with the traditional view. But while some such movement was apparent among the young and Latinos in 2008, a large panel study carried out by Polimetrix suggests that about two-thirds of the observed partisan change reflects movement by existing voters. Douglas Rivers, CEO of Polimetrix, personal conversation.

[35]Jacobson demonstrates that the national distribution of party identification clearly has been affected by evaluations of the performance of the Bush administration, although the duration of the effect naturally remains uncertain at this time. Gary Jacobson, "The Effects of the George W. Bush Presidency on Partisan Attitudes," *Presidential Studies Quarterly* 39 (2009), pp. 172–209.

[36]V. O. Key Jr., "A Theory of Critical Elections," *Journal of Politics* 17(1955), pp. 3–18. Walter Dean Burnham, *Critical Elections and the Mainsprings of American Politics* (New York, Norton: 1970). James Sundquist, *The Dynamics of the Party System: Alignment and Realignment of Poltiical Parties in the United States* (Washington, DC: Brookings, 1973).

[37]John B. Judis, "America the Liberal," *The New Republic*, November 5, 2008, http://www.tnr.com/article/politics/america-the-liberal (accessed October 29, 2009).

[38]A point emphasized in the treatment of realignments by Jerome M. Clubb, William H. Flanigan, and Nancy H. Zingale, *Partisan Realignment: Voters, Parties, and Government in American History* (Boulder, CO: Westview, 1990).

[39]David R. Mayhew, *Electoral Realignments: A Critique of an American Genre* (New Haven, CT: Yale, 2002).

[40]David W. Brady, *Critical Elections and Congressional Policy Making* (Stanford, CA: Stanford University Press, 1988).

[41]As the satirical newspaper, *The Onion* put it, "Black Man Given Nation's Worst Job," November 5, 2008, http://www.theonion.com/content/news_briefs/black_man_given_nations (accessed October 29, 2009).

[42]James Campbell has argued that if not for the September Wall Street meltdown, McCain would have won the election. But data from the Annenberg National Election Study, which interviewed large numbers of voters throughout the campaign, suggests that the campaign unfolded as predicted: Events like the stock market meltdown (and the Palin nomination) were epiphenomena. Seminar presentation by Richard Johnston, coprincipal investigator of ANES, February 27, 2009, Stanford University. cf. James E. Campbell, "An Exceptional Election: Performance, Values, and Crisis in the 2008 Presidential Election," *The Forum* 6(2008), Article 7, http://www.bepress.com/forum/vol6/iss4/art7/ (accessed October 29, 2009).

[43]"GOP Needs to Excommunicate its Heretics," *RealClearPolitcs*, November 10, 2008,

http://www.realclearpolitics.com/articles/2008/11/the_gop_needs_to_excommunicate.html (accessed October 29, 2009).

[44]Patrick J. Buchanan, "But Where Did Bush Go Wrong," *The American Standard*, November 4, 2008, http://buchanan.org/blog/pjb-but-where-did-bush-go-wrong-1268 (accessed October 29, 2009).

[45]See for example, Patrick J. Buchanan, "Return of the War Party, *The American Standard*, February 27, 2009, http://buchanan.org/blog/pjb-return-of-the-war-party-1463 (accessed October 29, 2009).

[46]William Kristol and David Brooks, "What Ails the Right?," *Wall Street Journal*, May 22, 2001, http://www.opinionjournal.com/extra/?id=95000513 (accessed October 29, 2009).

[47]Patrick J. Buchanan, "The Toyota Republicans," *The American Prospect*, December 16, 2008, http://buchanan.org/blog/pjb-the-toyota-republicans-1323 (accessed October 29, 2009).

[48]P. J. O'Rourke, "We Blew It," *The Weekly Standard*, November 17, 2008, http://www.weekly standard.com/Content/Public/Articles/000/000/015/791jsebl.asp (accessed October 29, 2009).

[49]Christine Todd Whitman and Robert M. Bostock, "Free the GOP," *Washington Post*, November 14, 2008.

[50]Kathleen Parker, "Giving Up on God," *Washington Post*, November 19, 2008, http://www.washingtonpost.com/wp-dyn/content/article/2008/11/18/AR2008111802886. html?nav%3Dhcmodule&sub=AR (accessed October 29, 2009).

[51]Jeffrey Hart, "the Christian Party," *The Daily Beast*, November 16, 2008, http://www.thedailybeast. com/blogs-and-stories/2008-11-16/the-christian-party/ (accessed October 29, 2009).

[52]Rod Dreher, "GOP's Path to Victory Still Goes Through God," *USA TODAY*, December 1, 2008.

[53]Ross Douthat, "Abortion Politics Didn't Doom the G.O.P.," *New York Times*, December 7, 2008, http://www.nytimes.com/2008/12/07/opinion/07douthat.html (accessed October 29, 2009).

[54]Ramesh Ponnuru, "Scapegoating the Social Right," *NRO*, December 16, 2008, http://nrd.nationalreview.com/article/?q=YTk3NTUxY2IxYmJkNjhhZjMyYzhhYzg1YjU1ZTk wZTY= (accessed October 29, 2009).

[55]"The Party of Sam's Club," *The Weekly Standard*, November 14, 2005.

http://www.weeklystandard.com/Content/Public/Articles/000/000/006/312korit.asp (accessed October 29, 2009).

[56]Michael Barone, "The GOP Should Go Upscale," *realclearpolitics.com*, http://www.realclear politics.com/articles/2009/02/the_gop_should_go_upscale.html (accessed October 29, 2009).

[57]Charlie Cook, "Learn or Languish, *National Journal*, November 15, 2008, http://www.cook political.com/node/4071 (accessed October 29, 2009).

[58]Lloyd A. Free and Hadley Cantril. *The Political Beliefs of Americans* (New Brunswick, NJ: Rutgers, 1967).

[59]Christopher Ellis and James A. Stimson, "Pathways to Ideology in American Politics: The Operational-Symbolic Paradox Revisited," Working Paper, University of North Carolina (forthcoming), at http://www.unc.edu.

[60]Clearly, the exact numbers would change from election to election and would vary with the issue questions that were included in the survey. The general conclusion—that self-identified conservatives are a much more heterogeneous lot than the much smaller category of self-iden-tified liberals—seems to us pretty solid, however.

[61]Quoted in Dreher, "GOP's Path to Victory Still Goes Through God."

[62]Morris P. Fiorina and Samuel J. Abrams, "Is California Really a Blue State?," in Frederick Douzet, Thad Kousser and Kenneth P. Miller, eds. *The New Political Geography of California* (Berkeley: Berkeley Public Policy Press, 2008), pp. 291–308.

[63]Mark I. Pinsky, "Meet the New Evangelicals," *Latimes.com*, September 16, 2006, http://arti-cles.latimes.com/2006/sep/16/opinion/oe-pinsky16 (accessed October 29, 2009). Lexington,

"Trouble in the Family, *The Economist*, March 3, 2007, p. 40. Albert Hunt, "Letter from Washington: Evangelical Christians Feared, but Multifaceted," *International Herald Tribune*, April 15, 2007. Nicholas D. Kristof, "Evangelicals a Liberal Can Love," *New York Times*, February 3, 2008, http://www.nytimes.com/2008/02/03/opinion/03kristof.html (accessed October 29, 2009). Michael Spencer, "The Coming Evangelical Collapse," *Christian Science Monitor*, March 10, 2009, http://www.csmonitor.com/2009/0310/p09s01-coop.html (accessed October 29, 2009).

[64]Kathleen Parker, "Political Pullback for the Christian Right?," *Washington Post*, April 5, 2009.

[65]Shortly after this chapter was written, James Dobson stepped down as the chairman of Focus on the Family, saying "One of the common errors of founder-presidents is to hold to the reins of leadership too long, thereby preventing the next generation from being prepared for executive authority." Quoted in Sarah Pulliam, "James Dobson Resigns from Focus on the Family," *Christianity Today*, February 27, 2009, http://blog.christianitytoday.com/ctliveblog/archives/2009/02/james_dobson_re.html (accessed October 29, 2009).

[66]As Gary Jacobson argues was the case in 1994. "The 1994 House Elections in Perspective," *Political Science Quarterly* 111(1996), pp. 203–23.

Chapter 2

How Barack Obama Changed Presidential Campaigns

David B. Magleby

"**C**hange" was the major theme of the Barack Obama presidential campaign. It was the only word to accompany his portrait on his most memorable campaign poster, and the answer to the implied action in his campaign refrain, "Yes We Can." Candidates from the party out of power commonly call for change, and in 2008 that theme had added resonance because of President George W. Bush's low standing in the polls and the unpopular Iraq War. But in Obama's case, his campaign represented change at several levels—including within his own party. As *Newsweek's* White House correspondent Richard Wolffe has observed, "Organizing voters. At the grassroots. For change. That was Obama's strategy from the outset as he mounted an audacious challenge to his own party and the political system."[1]

At a fundamental level the Obama candidacy embodied change because of his race. He was more competitive in the presidential nomination phase than any African American before him, even though he was running against experienced politicians like Senator John Edwards, Senator Joe Biden, Senator Chris Dodd, Senator Bill Richardson, and especially Senator Hillary Clinton. Senator Clinton's candidacy was itself historic, as she became the most prominent female contender yet to seek the nomination of a major party. She made history in a second way as the first spouse of a former president to seriously contend for the office. Clinton was the clear favorite as the race began.

It is important to note that unlike several other presidential contenders in both parties, Barack Obama was relatively untested as a candidate. He was first elected to the Illinois state legislature in 1996. He had run and lost in a race against an incumbent from his party for the U.S. House of Representatives in 2000. Four years later he secured the Democratic nomination in a crowded field in an open-seat contest to represent Illinois in the U.S. Senate. The general election contest for that seat had the makings of being a hotly contested race between Obama and Republican multimillionaire Jack Ryan. However, Ryan had to withdraw from the race because of a personal scandal and his Republican replacement, Alan Keyes, was essentially a stand-in, having unsuccessfully run twice for president and twice, in

Maryland, for a U.S. Senate seat.[2] Obama was not the first less-experienced candidate to run for office. Others, like Jimmy Carter, had done it before. Still, 2008 brought historic changes to the long-perceived gender and racial barriers in presidential nomination politics. And Barack Obama's campaign was remarkable for other reasons as well.

The Obama campaign departed from other campaigns in its use of the Internet and new media; in its approach to fundraising and the public campaign financing system; in the more widespread use of volunteers and the expanded number of field offices; in how it used voter data files for fundraising, organizing, communicating, and mobilizing voters in the nomination and general election phases; and in the expanded use of early and absentee voting. In some areas, the Obama campaign built on what others had done before, but on a larger scale and with a substantially different approach. In other areas, what the Obama campaign did was a fundamental departure from prior campaigns—a departure that will bring about another Obama "change" as it influences future presidential campaigns.

THE INTERNET AND NEW MEDIA

The Obama campaign's approach to technology, especially the Internet, was to weave it into all aspects of the campaign and use it much more extensively than had any prior campaign. In the words of Joe Rospars, who headed this part of the Obama campaign, the Internet was used to "integrate everything that was going on."[3] Obama made a clear and strong commitment early on to using technology to help identify, track, and mobilize supporters and voters. Rospars quantified Obama's support in terms of the numbers of paid staff working in this area, and in their proximity to the campaign's top leaders— even in the beginning, the technology group "was not just two folks sitting in the basement, but a group of 10-plus folks on the third floor outside the [campaign] chairman's office."[4] By the end of the campaign the number working in this area "rose to over one hundred."[5]

The innovations and changes in Internet usage by the Obama campaign were, in part, the result of what Dan Wagner described as the campaign's efforts to "leverage the power of really smart people."[6] For example, Rospars had worked for the 2004 Howard Dean presidential campaign and was a founding partner of Blue State Digital; another Obama supporter, Facebook cofounder Chris Hughes, took a leave of absence from his burgeoning company to work on the campaign.[7] Not surprisingly, the Obama campaign tapped into Facebook, accumulating 1.7 million Facebook supporters,[8] while nearly two million joined Obama's MySpace network or his state pages during the campaign.[9]

But the tool that set Obama apart was his Web site, My.BarackObama.com. This Web site, and other means, allowed his campaign to involve individuals in whatever mode of participation they desired—to volunteer, register to vote, talk to a friend, learn more about the candidate, download an Obama news widget, make a financial contribution, or receive phone numbers of voters across the country who needed to be called.[10] Political scientist Diana Owen describes these elements of the Obama campaign as "perhaps the most marked innovation."[11] The vision of the Obama Internet effort, according to Rospars, was to lower the "barriers to entry and make it as easy as possible for folks to come to our Web site."[12] A second objective was to raise "the expectation of what it means to be a supporter. It's not enough to have a bumper sticker. We want you to give five dollars, make some calls, and host an event. If you look at the messages we sent to people over time, there's a presumption that they will organize."[13]

Critical to the success of My.BarackObama.com was its design, which allowed individuals to take action on their own without direction or permission from the campaign. Campaigns generally want to control the message and determine the messenger. Obama exercised message control in advertising, but was less concerned about the content of person-to-person messages by supporters. Tools at My.BarackObama.com encouraged people to maintain personal profile pages, form affinity groups through listserv technology, network among friends, help to update calling lists, plan local events and prepare for caucuses, and to blog on the site while cross-posting blog entries on other sites, all with very little oversight.[14]

Candidates routinely use speeches and campaign events as a way to rally the troops and generate media coverage. The Obama campaign used events, large and small, to identify new supporters and recruit volunteers. At events, Obama often singled out his field staff for praise.[15] Those attending events were invited to fill out a card about themselves, their contact information including e-mail addresses and their issue concerns. This information became part of the Obama database for later contacts by the campaign, and the individuals received a text message or e-mail from Obama soon after the event, thanking them for coming and asking them for help with his campaign. While the events that drew large crowds gathered lots of attention, smaller events in community centers, schools, and homes may have been even more critical—especially in Iowa and other early deciding states. Such intimate events are not unusual, but the way Obama's campaign used the Internet to help identify people to invite, and then subsequently reinforce, was unusual.

As a result of these Internet and new media tools, the campaign learned about a much broader network of potential volunteers and donors. News sources estimated that Obama had 1.5 million active volunteers,[16] an e-mail list of 13 million,[17] and the campaign reported having 3 million Internet donors.[18] Many of these contacts were the result of friends telling friends, who in turn told others, a communications phenomenon sometimes called "viral."

The campaign's second objective, that of getting individuals to organize others, was also successful. Rospars noted that the campaign "had a thousand grassroots volunteer groups created in the first twenty-four hours after [Obama] announced [his campaign] on February 10, 2007."[19] Volunteers would in turn host house parties to recruit other volunteers, amassing 2,000 such parties by mid-2007.[20] These activities were important to Obama victories in nomination contests and in the general election. In the South Carolina primary for example, house parties hosted by African American women were important, and on that state's primary election day, 13,000 volunteers walked the streets to help get out the vote (including 2,000 out-of-state volunteers).[21]

Not surprisingly, the new technology tools were most frequently used by younger voters. This group, which historically votes less, was a major target for Obama in the Iowa caucuses and in every contest thereafter. The campaign achieved success among young voters. As campaign manager David Plouffe observed, "One of the more remarkable statistics of the entire election is that there were as many people under thirty as over sixty-five who caucused in the state of Iowa."[22]

An example of the creativity of the Obama campaign in engaging people in campaign activity is in the most highly attended Obama event of the primary campaign, a December 2007 outdoor rally featuring Oprah Winfrey at the University of South Carolina. At every entrance to the stadium, Obama volunteers distributed note cards to all adults as they entered. About 30 minutes before the event started, a young campaign staffer from the South Carolina headquarters asked everybody in the estimated crowd of 29,000 to use their cell phone to make calls to five South Carolina registered voters whose names and contact information were printed on the cards. Participants were asked to tell these prospective voters where they were and why they were supporting Barack Obama for president. When they completed this task, participants were asked to text message the campaign's five-digit number. Assuming only about half of those in attendance participated, the 15,000 who did could have reached 75,000 South Carolina primary voters in about 15 minutes.[23]

Obama changed campaigning in his much more extensive use of new media like YouTube. One prominent example was a song by will.i.am of the Black Eyed Peas, whose music video "Yes We Can" was viewed nearly 2 million times on YouTube in the first week,[24] and was viewed 14 million times on

YouTube by the end of the campaign.[25] In part due to this video, Obama's exposure on YouTube was estimated at a 29-to-1 advantage over McCain.[26] Many of the performers in "Yes We Can" were highly popular celebrities, including Scarlett Johansson, John Legend, and Herbie Hancock.[27]

Celebrities have long been a part of presidential campaigns, important for their endorsements and often used to help generate interest in campaign events. Mike Huckabee, the former Arkansas governor who ran in the 2008 Republican primaries, showcased Chuck and Gena Norris at campaign events, for example. But Obama invited celebrities to do more than provide an endorsement or appear at an event or in a video. They were asked to knock on doors, make phone calls, and contact people they knew, just as all campaign volunteers were.[28] The McCain campaign attempted to ridicule Obama as a "celebrity" candidate, with a negative ad featuring Paris Hilton, but the ad paled in impact compared to the personal involvement of individuals, including celebrities, in the Obama campaign.

FUNDRAISING

Obama did not start the 2007–08 election cycle as an experienced fundraiser on a national stage. Although he came from Illinois, a large state, Obama did not bring the kind of donor network to his race that George Bush or Al Gore did in 2000, or that other more established candidates did in 2008. The presumptive favorite for the nomination, [29] New York Senator Hillary Clinton, not only had the donor base she had cultivated in her New York campaigns, but could also build upon her husband's expansive donor base. One author described Bill Clinton as "Hillary's Rainmaker," contending that his "fundraising empire" was "perhaps the biggest payoff from the legacy of the 1990s."[30] Finally, it was anticipated that women would be especially likely to contribute to Senator Clinton's campaign with money and volunteer hours. An insurgent, or outside, candidate like Obama faced significant challenges, particularly in fundraising, as Richard Wolffe summarizes: "The headquarters, the consultants, the travel, the advance staff, the huge ground operation: it all needed vast sums of cash that no outsider had ever raised until they won a state or two. And by then, the infusion of dollars was typically too late: insurgent candidates always died at the first sign of life." [31]

Obama defied expectations by getting off to a very fast start in fundraising. His strategy was multifaceted. He established a network of donors who could give the legal maximum of $2,300 to his primary campaign. In 2007 he raised 33 percent of his money from donors giving at or near the maximum. This compared to 50 percent for Clinton and 23 percent for Edwards.[32] These early large contributions were important to establishing his credibility as a candidate, and in this part of his strategy he pursued a conventional approach, although as noted, he set new records with his success in fundraising in 2007.[33] The early money from large donors was raised through networks of established donors in a string of what one campaigner described as "back-to-back-to-back-to-back" events.[34] Wolffe writes that "contrary to their own carefully cultivated image, the money did not grow at the grass roots," nor on the Internet at first. "Internet donations totaled less than 15 percent of Obama's fundraising through 2007. Money only started to cascade through the Web after Iowa in early 2008, and it would take another several months, as the primaries dragged on, for the grassroots to represent half the campaign's early fundraising."[35]

Still, Obama's eventual success in online and small-donation fundraising has the potential to change campaigns going forward. Obama was not the first to try the Internet for raising campaign contributions. Howard Dean and Wesley Clark had enjoyed modest success using the Internet in 2004.[36] And John McCain had generated publicity in 2000 by raising $6.4 million via the Internet after winning the New Hampshire primary.[37] Some interest groups before 2007 had also seen success in raising money for particular causes via the Internet, most notably MoveOn.org, with its call to move past the Lewinsky scandal and, subsequently, with its opposition to the Iraq War.[38] But the Obama campaign used the Internet in fundraising in ways that went far beyond what anyone had done before. Obama campaign officials reported that "3 million donors gave 6.5 million donations for a total of more than $500 million online."[39] And Obama had extraordinary success among small donors, raising about one-third of the funds from people who gave under $200 to his campaign. This far surpassed what all other candidates raised via the Internet in 2007–08 or any earlier cycle. As Anthony Corrado observed, "No previous presidential contender had ever raised as much money through small contributions as Obama did."[40]

One strategy in raising small contributions drew criticism: the campaign's decision to not make fundraising a central component of its early involvement with people. Rospars explained that "When we first started, we actually left some money on the table by taking a little bit of time to show that we were interested in a total organizing relationship and laying out . . . the role we wanted supporters to play in the campaign. [T]hat allowed us to then introduce fundraising as part of that overall tone of relationship, which ultimately [earned] us more money in the end and a deeper relationship with our supporters."[41] This is not to say the Obama campaign did not eventually ask for money, because they did—but fundraising was not the major initial point of contact. Once a person became involved with the campaign in whatever way, they quickly received reinforcing communications from the campaign about events, issues, appearances, and the need for money. Thank-you e-mails, with the tone of personal notes, came variously from Barack Obama, David Plouffe, Michelle Obama, and after he was selected as the running mate, Joe Biden. And once individuals had given electronically, they were added to a database of likely future donors.

Obama's success in fundraising through the Internet was partly due to his persona, partly due to his message, and partly due to his willingness to embrace the capacity of the Internet. Obama was a dynamic, articulate, and historic candidate. He demonstrated remarkable presence during the campaign and engaged his audience, including the television audience. His antiwar message won early support. Unlike the other leading candidates—Clinton and Edwards—and unlike John Kerry in 2004, Obama had a consistent record of opposition to the war in Iraq. In the early going of the fundraising effort, especially among small donors, Obama's opposition to the Iraq War was a distinguishing characteristic. Reporters Dan Balz and Haynes Johnson observe that "of all the candidates, Obama had staked out the earliest, clearest and most eloquently expressed opposition to the war."[42] And as MoveOn.org had demonstrated, a network of people had already contributed online to an interest group opposed to the war—a network Obama could tap.[43] Beyond fundraising, his use of the Internet allowed him to maximize his message and persona.

Raising money via the Internet has a lot of advantages. Asking for money through the mail takes longer, is much more expensive, and requires a waiting period for checks to clear the bank. By contrast, campaigns can put online contributions to immediate use. Raising money at an event like a dinner or concert also means the money from that event may not get to the campaign for some days, while the costs associated with the dinner or concert must be deducted. As a result, not all money contributed can be used by the campaign. Raising money at events also takes the candidate away from campaigning, and because the candidate needs to go to different places to hold the events, the travel time is a further distraction. Alternatively, it only takes a few minutes to draft a new e-mail request for funds. Because it is so inexpensive to use the Internet to raise money, individuals who can only make $5 contributions can still be profitably solicited, and people making contributions to Obama at all levels via the Internet were invited to give again and again. Some individuals even set up automatic withdrawals on a regular basis from their bank account.

Asking for money can be much more timely and immediate via the Internet. The campaign used events that would naturally generate interest in supporters to make repeat solicitations. The candidate debates, the need to do well in next week's primaries, or responses to an attack from an opponent were all fodder for the e-mail solicitations. One especially effective "ask" came on the night of the Rudolph Giuliani and Sarah Palin speeches at the GOP convention. Campaign media director Joe Rospars relates what happened: "When she [Palin] questioned Obama's qualifications for office as limited to being only a community organizer, the Obama campaign saw a spike in online donation. . . . The first line of the e-mail to supporters or staff from David Plouffe was, 'I was not planning on writing to you tonight but I cannot believe what I just saw' and outlined what had happened." Rospars further reported that the Obama campaign received about $12 million over the 24 hours after Palin's acceptance speech, the largest amount in any single day of the campaign.[44] Similarly, campaign manager David Plouffe viewed Palin as "a big multiplier. We were going to have a big September no matter what. But she probably was worth at least $20 million, $25 million, I would guess."[45] Obama was not the first candidate to use many of these approaches, but he is clearly the most successful in using the Internet for fundraising.

Campaigns have long relied on well-connected individuals to solicit funds from friends and people they know. These fundraisers are sometimes called "bundlers" because they may present the campaign with a bundle of checks totaling $100,000 or more. The Obama campaign had bundlers in this conventional sense, but it also encouraged what might be called "microbundlers," individuals who asked their friends and colleagues to contribute even at small levels. The campaign added to this approach the idea of the initial donor or microbundler matching the contributions of those they solicited up to a set amount.

Obama changed fundraising in another way as well. He was the first major party general election candidate since public financing was initiated in 1976 to not take public funds in lieu of continued fundraising in the general election. Even candidates like Ronald Reagan and George W. Bush, who were generally critical of government solutions and programs, nevertheless took public funding, at least for the general election. Obama had emphasized throughout his campaign that he wanted to fundraise directly from individuals as much as possible and especially from many individuals making small contributions. He made a point of declining contributions from federal lobbyists and political action committees (PACs).[46]

Early in the campaign Obama had pledged to "aggressively pursue an agreement with the Republican nominee to pursue a publicly financed general election."[47] Obama reversed himself on his pledge despite the fact that John McCain, his GOP opponent, had announced he would accept public funds. Obama explained his reversal by praising his fans: "You've fueled this campaign with donations of $5, $10, and $20, whatever you can afford. . . . And because you did, we've built a grassroots movement of over 1.5 million Americans."[48] Obama also justified his decision as a move to counteract the spending of his opponent, the Republican Party, and 527 organizations. (Interest groups organized under section 527 of the Internal Revenue Code are called 527 organizations.) Such groups had been active and important in the 2000 and 2004 elections.[49] Obama said, "John McCain's campaign and the Republican National Committee are fueled by contributions from Washington lobbyists and special interest PACs. And we've already seen that he's not going to stop the smears and attacks from his allies running so-called 527 groups, who will spend millions and millions of dollars in unlimited donations."[50]

Figure 1. Money Raised by McCain, Bush, Kerry, Obama and Their National Party Committees Over Time

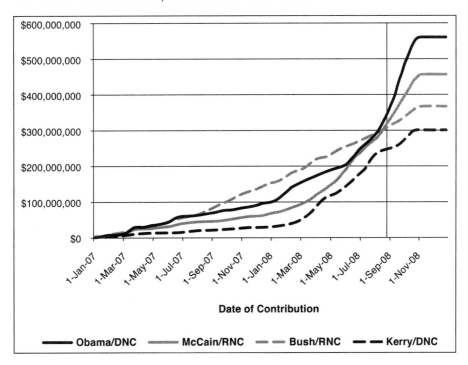

Source: FEC records of individual contributions, downloaded March 3, 2009. Reprinted from David B. Magleby, Bradley Jones, and David Lassen, "Turning the Tables: Individual Contributions, Member Contributions, and the Changing Campaign Finance Environment," *The Forum* 7, no.1 (2009).

Note: The vertical line near the beginning of September 2008 indicates the approximate date of the national party conventions. All amounts are in 2008 dollars.

Obama took some risks by declining public funds in the general election. What if his donor pool stopped growing or ceased to continue to give? Had he been forced to raise money through dinners and events, he would have had less time for other campaign activities and would have been diverted from battleground states to places where Democrats often raise money—California and New York, where he already had a substantial lead in the polls. At the same time, the large amount of money that Obama had left over from the primaries made this decision less risky. Figure 1 plots money raised by McCain and Obama in 2008 and by Bush and Kerry in 2004, along with the fundraising of their respective national party committee.

As it turned out, Obama's fundraising only accelerated in September and October, as Figure 1 demonstrates. In September he raised over $150 million,[51] which meant his campaign could continue to aggressively advertise and compete in states not pursued by Kerry in 2004 or Gore in 2000. As a result of Obama's success in raising money during the general election campaign, future nominees will likely follow his example and decline public funding. Bill McInturff, a pollster for the McCain campaign, implicates Obama with the end of public financing: "Senator Obama's decision has destroyed the campaign finance system forever. No Republican will ever be able to run and take even primary money because [they'll] be outspent. The public finance system worked pretty well, so that . . . lots of candidates could get in with a fairly low cost of change, get matching money, and run a credible campaign. Those people won't exist anymore. You are going to have to start with the capacity to raise an extraordinary amount of money, and it will change the presidential field."[52]

Obama's success in raising money from individuals in small and large amounts gave his campaign tremendous advantages in radio and television advertising and beyond. James A. Thurber writes that Obama was able to "dominate all aspects of the media 'air war': television, cable, radio, direct mail, and even advertising in video games."[53] Obama and the Democratic National Committee (DNC) spent $236.6 million on television ads compared to $126 million by McCain and the Republican National Committee (RNC).[54] Obama had enough money to run ads on network programs, including during football games, and even to purchase 30 minutes of network television for an infomercial that delayed the start of a World Series baseball game by 15 minutes.[55]

In many ways the 2004 election was a repeat of the 2000 election, with a set of predictable Republican (Red) states and a set of predictably Democratic (Blue) states, and a small number of battleground states determining the outcome. Early indications were that this would again be the case in 2008. But a combination of Obama's popularity, especially among African Americans and young voters,[56] and his having run nomination battles in all states, and his money advantage, meant he could add states to the "toss-up" column that were not toss-ups in 2000 or 2004, such as North Carolina, Indiana, and Virginia.[57] Obama's money advantage also helped him expand the playing field and change the dynamic of the 2008 election. When the campaign decided to contest a state, they did so aggressively. As the campaign's national field director, Jon Carson put it, "If we were in, we put in the resources needed to win."[58] This was a change from other campaigns in that the campaign was not trying to stem the tide in a set of states, they were self-consciously trying to create and maintain their own tidal wave.

A COMMUNITY ORGANIZER CHANGES THE GROUND GAME

The Obama campaign's success in fundraising in many respects made possible its innovations in other parts of campaigning, like the simultaneous large investment in the ground game and in conventional advertising. Obama's money advantage allowed him to have a much larger number of field offices than McCain and the RNC, which in turn helped him harness the energy of his larger number of volunteers. But what was unusual about the Obama campaign is how he applied to a presidential campaign lessons learned as a community organizer. Richard Wolffe, who traveled extensively with Obama during the campaign and visited many field offices, describes the connection as follows: "Community organizing lay at the heart of their game plan in Iowa, the character of the campaign, [and] his philosophy as a politician. . . . It would shape the candidate and his quest through the presidency for the entire election cycle."[59]

Whether being a community organizer is solid preparation for some aspects of the presidency is debatable, but it turned out to be excellent training for Obama in building a large-scale, community-based presidential campaign.

Central to a successful campaign is identifying and tracking individuals at varying levels of commitment. Databases are vital to this function. As Jon Carson said, "As a community organizer himself, he knew the value of a list and the value of using every opportunity to get that work done."[60] Volunteers were an important element of the Obama campaign, both in voter tracking and voter contacting. All campaigns rely on volunteers, but the Obama campaign demonstrated exceptional creativity in recruiting volunteers and giving them meaningful tasks to perform. Dennis Johnson, an experienced observer of campaigns, writes that "the Obama campaign, more so than any 2008 or previous presidential campaign, emphasized a special relationship with its supporters."[61]

The volunteer effort, especially as orchestrated and overseen by the field offices, was critical to Obama's victory. Carson reports that while the campaign benefited from individuals doing their own contacting via the Internet, "the vast bulk of voter contact that is done is done the old fashioned way, with organizers and volunteers putting lists in the hands of volunteers."

Much of the volunteer activity was orchestrated and coordinated through field offices in every state. The campaign has not released an official number of field offices and estimates vary, but a reasonable estimate would be that by the end of the general election the campaign had over 770 field offices.[62] A study of five states identified before the election as likely to be competitive offers more precise comparison figures on the numbers of field offices in the McCain and Obama general election campaigns. In these battlegrounds, at least, Obama offices outnumbered McCain offices two to one. [63] Table 1 presents these data for the five states.

Obama's experience as a community organizer was directly relevant to the task of organizing volunteers in communities to assist with his campaign. Key to the organizing strategy was a cadre of trained staff deployed early on who managed the local field offices. The goal was "to give their young field

Table 1. Number of Obama and McCain Offices in Five Sample States, 2008

	CO	NC	NH	NM	OH
Obama	50	47	19	38	89
McCain	12	20	14	18	45
Total	62	67	33	56	134

Sources: Jeremy Pelzer, "McCain Advisers Give Up on Colorado," *Politicker.com*, http://www.politicker.com/colorado/5696/cnn-mccain-advisers-give-colorado; Jim Tankersley and Christi Parsons, "Fundraising a Big Advantage for Obama," *Chicago Tribune*, October 20, 2008; Obama for President, "Campaign for Change Regional Field Offices: Colorado," http://my.barackobama.com/page/content/cooffices/, (accessed April 13, 2009); Obama for President, "Campaign for Change Regional Field Offices: New Hampshire," http://my.barackobama.com/page/content/nhoffices/, (accessed April 13, 2009); Obama for President, "Campaign for Change Regional Field Offices: New Mexico," http://my.barackobama.com/page/content/nmoffices/, (accessed April 13, 2009); Obama for President, "Campaign for Change Regional Field Offices: North Carolina," http://my.barackobama.com/page/ content/ncoffices/, (accessed April 13, 2009); Obama for President, "Campaign for Change Regional Field Offices: Ohio," http://my.barackobama.com/page/ content/ohoffices/, (accessed April 13, 2009); Eric Dienstfrey, "NM: Obama 45, McCain 40," *Pollster.com*, October 6, 2008, http://www.pollster.com/blogs/ nm_obama_45_mccain_40_albuqjou.php, (accessed April 13, 2009).

organizers a chance to set down roots in the community."[64] These field staffers were trained in "Camp Obama," a two- to four-day training event for those who wanted to be activists in the campaign.[65] Marshall Ganz, a Harvard professor whom Obama enlisted to assist in his campaign, summarized the approach as follows: "Organizing combines the language of the heart as well as the head."[66] Others have noted that Camp Obama was one of the first signs that "Obama's campaign [had] embodied many of the characteristics of a social movement."[67]

Training volunteers before deploying them to the field instilled a sense of shared purpose. In its scale and scope this training was a change from other presidential campaigns. By the end of 2007 Obama had 159 paid staffers in Iowa supported by 10,000 volunteers.[68] Training allowed the Obama headquarters team to be sure the deployed field staff understood campaign priorities, protocols, and such matters as database management. These paid staffers managed a range of activities in the office, including training volunteers for tasks like telephoning undecided voters, helping process voter registration forms, answering incoming phone calls about where to vote or how to volunteer, or preparing volunteers to be precinct observers.

With the expectation that they would be with the campaign for the duration, Obama field staff were paid about $2,000 a month—significantly less than Clinton's or Edwards's field staff (at $2,500 and $2,700, respectively). [69] A similar gap in wages for Obama staff existed at more senior levels.[70] In a campaign that generated so many volunteers, it may have been possible to have had fewer paid staff, but paying the staff conveyed a sense of mutual commitment. Many of Obama's field staffers lived in the homes of campaign volunteers, which meant the campaign could pay them less. The field staff were typically young, often recent college graduates or college students who took time off from school.

One of the advantages Obama's campaign had over McCain's and prior Democratic campaigns is that many of the field staff had managed field offices during the nomination phase of the campaign, sometimes in more than one primary or caucus, before managing a field office in the general election. McCain had effectively secured the nomination by February 7, 2008, after only 33 states had held caucuses or primaries.[71] In contrast, Obama and Clinton were in a tight race to the Democratic nomination with real contests in all fifty states and all U.S. territories. This meant the Obama field operation was more experienced and tested than McCain's. It also meant more grassroots support for the whole Democratic ticket. In a study of the 2008 elections in North Carolina, which has a late primary, Eric Heberlig, Peter Francia, and Steven Greene report that Obama's statewide organization during the nomination phase "brought with it the potential to mobilize thousands of first-time, young, and minority voters for down-ballot candidates in November."[72]

Reporting and accountability were important to the field operation. Field staff participated in daily telephone conference calls with other paid staff in their region and occasionally their state. The regional offices and the national campaign offices in Chicago received daily reports on each office's numbers of voters registered, contacted in person, and contacted by phone. Offices also functioned as a place for people to walk in to secure a bumper sticker or yard sign, or to volunteer. The person who greeted this drop-in traffic was often the paid staff member, who answered questions and inquired about possible interest in helping the campaign. If the answer was affirmative, the visitor completed a form specific to the volunteer task and was informed of when the next training for that task would be conducted. All of this information was entered into the campaign's database.

One of the advantages the Obama campaign had in both the primaries and general election was more energy among supporters, often described as an "enthusiasm gap." Dan Balz and Haynes Johnson contrast Obama and Clinton in the primaries: "Perhaps most critical of all, [Clinton] was never able to match the energy and enthusiasm that Obama inspired among new young voters. With his change message, Obama struck a unique chord."[73]

The field offices were in generally visible and central locations, often in places that previously had been used as restaurants or stores, or may not have been rented for some time. In some cases, the space for the field offices was paid for by local volunteers or contributed as an in-kind campaign donation.[74] The furnishings were not uniform or new. Common elements of the field offices were the hand-painted Obama signs facing the street and children's art in the entrance area. Richard Wolffe describes an Iowa field office: "Obama's headquarters were a cross between a college dorm, community center, and personality cult. On the wall of the reception desk was a motto that sounded more suited to the side of a police cruiser: Respect, Empower, Include. Opposite was a rendering of Grant Wood's *American Gothic*, with the elderly couple holding a sign saying "Obama for America" instead of a pitchfork."[75]

The functions of the field offices were not different from other campaigns. Common to all modern campaigns are computers and printers, telephones, and photocopiers.

An example of the greater focus of staff and volunteers at Obama's field offices was the general absence of televisions, compared to their frequent presence in McCain's field offices. When asked about this distinction, one paid field staffer said, "We did not have time to watch television. We wanted to make news, not watch the news."[76]

VOTER FILES, MICROTARGETING, AND TURNOUT

Campaigns have always needed to track individual voter preferences and tailor campaign efforts accordingly. Political scientists sometimes describe the public from the perspective of the candidate as "saints, sinners, and savables."[77] Candidates presumably reinforce their relations with the "saints" and try to win over as many "savables" as possible, while not worrying much about the "sinners." In today's campaigns, candidates have much more precise data on who is registered to vote and who is not, on who has voted in the past and in what kinds of elections, on party registration in states where that is allowed, on group affiliations, consumer preferences, and so on. All of this becomes part of a large voter file maintained by the campaign.

In the 2004 election, the Republicans were more skilled than the Democrats in computer modeling of where to go to find more voters. The RNC had developed a superior voter file in terms of current and accurate information on voters, including individual characteristics like whether they had hunting or fishing licenses, subscribed to particular publications, or had voted in primary elections over several years. This data was used to target individuals who had moved but not registered at their new address or to communicate particular appeals about a candidate or the party. This process is called microtargeting.[78]

Democratic voter registration and mobilization in 2004 was largely done by America Coming Together (ACT). An outside group organized under section 527 of the IRS Code, it was funded by wealthy individuals like George Soros, Peter Lewis, and Stephen Bing,[79] as well as by organized labor and other progressive interest groups. ACT expanded the voter rolls and in many states helped Democrats exceed their turnout targets, but they still lost the election.[80] Prior to 2004, Democrats relied on microtargeting and Get-Out-the-Vote efforts by individual interest group allies, and on activities of the DNC, funded in part by "soft money"—the unlimited money party committees can raise from individuals, corporations, and unions for party building purposes. Republicans have long done their voter registration and mobilization through the RNC, and this was again the case in 2008.

Unlike the 2004 Kerry campaign, the Obama campaign did its own voter registration and mobilization. The campaign made extensive use of databases and microtargeting by adding and updating data on voters through its own database, developed during the nomination. Data collected by field offices and on the campaign Web site was particularly valuable as the list of battle-ground states grew. The Obama campaign worked to register voters, get them to participate in caucuses and primaries, and then to vote in the general election. All of these activities involved microtargeting on a scale not seen in any prior Democratic presidential campaign, and rivaling that of the Bush campaign in 2004.

At the same time, Obama's allies were important to his success in microtargeting. Growing out of ACT's large-scale voter registration and mobilization effort in 2004 came a new strategy in 2005 and 2006 to form a corporation that would build a superior voter file and foster a culture of social science modelers to compete with the Republicans' file. Harold Ickes, Clinton White House chief of staff and Hillary Clinton devotee, orchestrated fundraising for the group that built the database, initially named the "Data Warehouse,"[81] and later known as "Catalist." By the 2008 election cycle the quality and size of the Catalist voter file was on par with the Republicans' voter file and in some respects may have been superior to it.

The Democrats have an advantage, which Catalist is designed to maximize: more interest group and union support. Catalist's data partners include several large membership organizations, including unions, such as the National Education Association (NEA), and pro-choice and environmental groups. These groups were constantly updating the Catalist list and providing new information to the file. Both the Clinton and later the Obama campaign purchased the Catalist file, which they merged with their own voter file, providing additional valuable information for modeling which persons to contact and with what messages. Ken Strasma, a computer modeler who worked on the Obama campaign, said of the Obama campaign, "microtargeting was very important . . . in caucus states. So, you have a lot of people who were instrumental in pulling the surprise . . . for Obama, [who] were very invested in microtargeting. So when it came the time to be planning the general election, we didn't have to do any kind of selling job or persuading people that it was valuable."[82] Obama changed the way presidential candidates do voter registration and mobilization by fully integrating these key functions into his campaign.

Unlike many Western democracies with permanent voter registration, the United States requires voters to register again whenever they move, or if they have not voted in a recent election. Many voters do not meet this expectation. Individuals who are less likely to be registered include the young, who are highly mobile, the less educated and less affluent, who may lack self-confidence in dealing with bureaucracy, and those who just feel like their vote will not matter. For a candidate like Barack Obama, getting these supporters registered was a key component of the campaign. Identifying such voters was aided by the merged campaign and Catalist data files.

Aware of some past problems with interest group voter registration efforts, the campaign worked with local election officials to clarify expectations for completed voter registration forms. Evidence of the success of the campaign in registering voters is found in the fact that an estimated 3.5 million people registered to vote for the first time during the primary,[83] and in a Wall Street Journal poll taken in late October, reporting that 69 percent of new or lapsed voters planned to vote for Obama.[84] Expanding the voter rolls was critical to the Obama campaign's goal of bringing more states into play in the general election.[85]

Another critical element was getting those registered voters to turn out to caucus and vote. Getting people to participate in a caucus is more difficult than getting them to vote at the polls on Election Day. Participation at a caucus requires a voter to go to a specified location at a specified time, usually in the evening, and may require them to be part of a public meeting prior to voting, in which they may have to publicly indicate support for their candidate of choice. In comparison, getting a voter to the polls can occur generally any time over a 13- or 14-hour period, and there is no expectation beyond the waiting in line to enter a booth, where a voter casts a secret ballot in private. The Obama campaign won 13 of the 14 caucus states in 2008, losing only Nevada to Clinton. They did this through superior voter mobilization, and clear communication via the Web and in-person about what participation in a caucus requires, and where each supporter would caucus. Obama campaign manager, David Plouffe, commented on the advantages of this tool: "In Iowa, we had over twenty thousand people, in the last few days, go to that caucus lookup tool, so we knew who those people were. Some of them were undecided, so it was an opportunity to talk to them. Given that we had to expand the electorate, it was remarkable to see, time and time again, that there were a lot of people out there who did not know how to participate."[86]

Moreover, as Joe Rospars noted, when individuals looked up their polling location on the Obama site, the campaign "provided five other people according to our voter file database with e-mail and phone numbers whom you could take with you to the polls."[87] As with other elements of the campaign, the protracted primary battle between Clinton and Obama gave the Obama campaign ample opportunity to learn how to maximize voter turnout.

The 2008 general election saw a substantial increase in the availability of early voting and "no-excuse" absentee voting. Both processes require extra steps on the voter's part, and here, as with caucus participation, the Obama campaign exploited its organizational and field advantage to secure more votes. In the wake of the 2000 ballot counting controversy in Florida and the long lines in some Ohio counties in 2004, many states developed provisions to allow voting on specified days before Election Day, at a smaller number of locations. Early voting lessens the pressure on poll workers and local election officials by allowing a substantial fraction of the vote to be cast early.

Past campaigns have sometimes spent scarce resources on mobilizing "high propensity" voters, meaning voters likely to vote on Election Day, to vote early. Such efforts are seen as an inefficient use of campaign resources. The Obama campaign used computer models to identify "low propensity" voters and persuade them to vote early, relying on the high propensity voters to decide for themselves whether they voted early or not. As reporters Balz and Johnson summarize, the Obama campaign's goal "was to bank as many votes as possible before election day—especially voters who were newly registered or had participated only sporadically in the past."[88] David Plouffe said, "You keep communicating to the recent converts, but you turn more to conversion about getting them to vote. We put a huge priority on getting people who converted early to vote early, if the state allowed that."[89] Voters who waited until Election Day to vote still received reminder calls or e-mails from the campaign on Election Day, but the focus of the Obama early voting effort was on low propensity voters. How well did the campaign do in mobilizing these voters? As noted, exit polls report that of first-time voters, 69 percent voted for Obama.

Another way people can vote early is by requesting an absentee ballot, completing it at home, and mailing it in before the election. Only a few years ago, voters in many states had to claim a particular reason for requesting an absentee ballot. But since 2000 states have typically abandoned that requirement and substituted what is called "no-excuse" absentee voting. In some states, such as Oregon, voters now vote almost entirely through the mail, while in others, like Washington and California, many vote by mail or vote early. Early and absentee voting were important. In North Carolina, for example, Obama carried the state by fewer than 13,000 votes and McCain soundly carried Election Day voting. It was only the disparity in early voting (1,382,199 for Obama and 1,077,145 for McCain) that swayed the state into Obama's column.

The Obama campaign was not responsible for the changes in the law that permit voters to vote early or by absentee, but the Obama campaign, more than any other campaign to date, exploited these provisions—as well as the public information regarding voters who have requested and returned an absentee ballot or voted early. Using their superior field operation, voter file, and database management, they carefully tracked which likely Obama supporters had requested an absentee ballot and whether that ballot had yet been received at the county clerk's office. If it had not been received, reminder e-mails or phone calls went out until it was received. For a data-driven campaign like Obama's, early voting and absentee voting has the additional benefit of reducing the number of voters remaining to target on Election Day.

As in the caucuses and primaries, the Obama campaign demonstrated in the lead up to Election Day, and on Election Day itself, a capacity to mobilize people beyond what any campaign has done to date. Communications with voters were personalized with information on the precinct in which the voter lived, the voting location for that precinct, and what hours it was open. But as with so much of the Obama campaign, mobilization was a person-to-person phenomenon. Balz and Johnson describe that during the "final weekend Obama supporters knocked on more than four million doors in Pennsylvania [and] almost half a million the Saturday before the election in Ohio, while in California volunteers placed a million calls into other states and poured into neighboring Nevada to knock on more doors. Illinois volunteers flooded into Wisconsin, Indiana, Iowa, and Missouri."[90]

Exit polls and the National Election Study (NES) both find that respondents were more likely to have been contacted by the Obama campaign than by the McCain campaign. In 2008, 19 percent of respondents in the media exit poll reported having been contacted by McCain's campaign, down 5 percent from the proportion in 2004 who reported having been contacted by George W. Bush's campaign. Interestingly, an identical 26 percent reported having been contacted by the Kerry campaign in 2004 and the Obama campaign in 2008.[91]

As noted, McCain lacked the resources and his party lacked the enthusiasm to compete with Obama and his allies.

IMPLICATIONS FOR THE FUTURE OF CAMPAIGNING

The Obama campaign benefited from being able to run at a time when the Republican "brand" was unpopular generally, especially in the persona of President George W. Bush. As a candidate, Obama had a compelling story that resonated with many Americans. But it is also the case that the Obama campaign was well organized, well funded, and disciplined. Joe Trippi, who had been campaign manager for the 2004 Howard Dean campaign and was an advisor to the John Edwards campaign in 2007–08, said of the Obama campaign, "He did everything better . . . it's like the Dean campaign were the Wright brothers, the Obama campaign was *Apollo 11*, and we've skipped everything in between."[92] In strategy and in technological innovation, Obama changed the way presidential candidates are likely to campaign in the future.

Building on Obama's success, serious candidates for president will not likely again take public funds. They will probably cultivate and rely on small Internet donors side-by-side with large individual contributors, while promoting social networking-type involvement through more interactive Web sites. Mobilization and microtargeting made substantial strides in 2004 and progressed further in 2008. It is reasonable to assume that future presidential elections will see even greater use of databases in microtargeting, although it may be difficult to duplicate the level of enthusiasm seen among the Obama supporters who used that data to do the actual contacting.

How generalizable the Obama campaign is to congressional or state and local campaigns is debatable. Not all candidates have the candidate appeal Obama had. Few have the capacity to amass the start-up resources he generated. Whether the Internet can be used by candidates at all levels as a tool for mobilizing, persuading, and fundraising remains to be seen. But serious candidates at all levels will certainly give the Internet a serious try.

QUESTIONS TO CONSIDER

1. In what ways did Obama's experience as a community organizer influence his campaign style?
2. How did the Obama campaign use new technology to mobilize voters, volunteers, and donors?
3. Do you think the innovations of the Obama campaign can be successfully used in other campaigns? How? Why?

NOTES

[1] Richard Wolffe, *Renegade: the Making of a President* (New York: Crown Publishers, 2009), p. 67.

[2] Associated Press, "Report: Keyes Will Accept GOP Nomination, Run Against Obama," August 6, 2004, http://www.lexisnexis.com/us/lnacademic/results/docview/docview.do?doc LinkInd=true&risb=21_T7128573479&format=GNBFI&sort=RELEVANCE&startDocNo= 1&resultsUrlKey=29_T7128573482&cisb=22_T7128573481&treeMax=true&treeWidth=0 &csi=304478&docNo=1 (accessed August 11, 2009).

[3] Joe Rospars, Obama for America new media director, interview by David Magleby, January 28, 2009.

[4] Ibid.

[5] Ibid.

[6] Dan Wagner, DNC national targeting director, remarks at *The Change Election* Press Event, Washington, D.C., June 23, 2009.

[7] Joshua Green, "The Amazing Money Machine," *The Atlantic*, June 2008, http://www.theatlantic.com/doc/200806/obama-finance (accessed September 15, 2009).

[8] Samuel Greengard, "The First Internet President," *Communications of the ACM* 52, no. 2 (February 2009).

[9]Mike Unger, "Obama's Media Guru Brings Message to Campaign Management Institute," *American Today*, January 2009, http://veracity.univpubs.american.edu/today/vol/12/6/012109-obama-campaign-newmedia.html (accessed September 15, 2009).

[10]Green, "The Amazing Money Machine."

[11]Diana Owen, "The Campaign and the Media," in Janet M. Box-Steffensmeier and Steven E. Schier, *The American Elections of 2008* (Lanham, MD: Rowman & Littlefield), p. 9.

[12]Joe Rospars, Obama For America new media director, qtd. in Green, "The Amazing Money Machine."

[13]Ibid.; see also Greengard, "The First Internet President."

[14]Geoff Norquay, "Organizing Without an Organization: The Obama Networking Revolution," *Policy Options*, October 2008, p. 59.

[15]Wolffe, *Renegade*, p. 82.

[16]John Berman, "Obama Supporters Without a Cause," *ABC News*, November 15, 2008, http://abcnews.go.com/GMA/Weekend/story?id=6258425 (accessed September 22, 2009).

[17]Balz and Johnson, *Battle*, pp. 365–66.

[18]Vargas, "Obama Raised Half A Billion Online," *washingtonpost.com*, November 20, 2008, http://voices.washingtonpost.com/44/2008/11/20/obama_raised_half_a_billion_on.html (accessed September 1, 2009).

[19]Balz and Johnson, *Battle*, pp. 184–85.

[20]Ibid., p. 165.

[21]Ibid.

[22]David Plouffe, qtd. in Institute of Politics, John F. Kennedy School of Government at Harvard University, *Campaign for President: The Managers Look at 2008* (Lanham, MD: Rowman & Littlefield, 2009), p. 125.

[23]Vargas, "Obama Raised a Half Billion Online."

[24]Associated Press, "Viral Video Features Celebrities, Obama Mantra 'Yes, We Can,'" February 6, 2008, http://www.foxnews.com/politics/elections/2008/02/06/viral-video-features-celebrities-obama-mantra-yes-we-can/ (accessed September 15, 2009).

[25]Dana Coffield, Stephen Keating, and Tucker Shaw, "Pop Culture Moments on the Campaign Trail," *Denver Post*, November 4, 2008.

[26]Micah L. Sifry, "How Much is YouTube Worth to Obama and McCain?" October 24, 2008, http://techpresident.com/node/6454 (accessed September 15, 2009).

[27]Jay Newton-Small, "Obama's Celebrity Army," *Time.com*, February 4, 2008, http://www.time.com/time/politics/article/0,8599,1709745,00.html (accessed August 14, 2009).

[28]Ibid.

[29]David S. Broder, "The Making of a Front Runner," *Washington Post*, September 6, 2007, http://www.washingtonpost.com/wp-dyn/content/article/2007/09/05/AR2007090502043.html (accessed September 14, 2009).

[30]Daviel Nichanian, "Bill Clinton: Hillary's Rainmaker," *Huffington Post*, November 20, 2007, http://www.huffingtonpost.com/daniel-nichanian/bill-clinton-hillarys-rai_1_b_75323.html (accessed September 17, 2009).

[31]Wolffe, *Renegade*, pp. 71–72.

[32]David B. Magleby, "Rolling in the Dough: The Continued Surge in Individual Contributions to Presidential Candidates and Party Committees," *The Forum: A Journal of Applied Research in Contemporary Politics* 6, no.1, article 5 (2008), p. 9, http://www.bepress.com/forum/vol6/iss1/art5 (accessed October 23, 2009).

[33]Ben Smith and Richard Allen Greene, "Obama, Clinton Smash Fundraising Records," July 1, 2007, *Politico*, http://www.politico.com/news/stories/0707/4747.html (accessed September 16, 2009).

[34]Penny Pritzer, national finance chair, Obama for America, qtd. in Wolffe, *Renegade*, pp. 74–75. Wolffe observes that large donors were another group Obama sought to organize for activities beyond fundraising (p. 20).

[35]Wolffe, *Renegade*, pp. 74–75.

[36]Greengard, "The First Internet President"; see also Anthony Corrado, "Financing the Presidential Nomination Campaigns," *Financing the 2004 Election* (Washington, DC: Brookings Institution Press, 2006), p. 115.

[37]Dennis W. Johnson, *Routledge Handbook of Political Management* (New York: Taylor & Francis, 2008), p. 167.

[38]Formed by Wes Boyd and Joan Blade, MoveOn continues to use the Internet to raise money and call for policies it favors. See Public Citizen, "Overview: MoveOn.org," http://www.stealthpacs.org/profile.cfm?org_id=218 (accessed September 16, 2009).

[39]Vargas, "Obama Raised Half A Billion Online."

[40]Anthony Corrado, "Fund-raising Strategies in the 2008 Presidential Campaign," in *Campaigns and Elections American Style*, 3rd ed. (Boulder, CO: Westview Press, 2009), p. 114.

[41]Joe Rospars, Obama for America new media director, interview by David Magleby, January 28, 2009.

[42]Balz and Johnson, *Battle*, p. 22.

[43]Jeff Zeleny and Patrick Healy, "Obama Wins Endorsement of MoveOn.org," *New York Times*, February 2, 2008, http://query.nytimes.com/gst/fullpage.html?res=9E06E0D81F3CF931 A35751C0A96E9C8B63 (accessed September 16, 2009).

[44]Joe Rospars, Obama for America new media director, interview by David Magleby, January 28, 2009; for a lower estimate of the money raised in that period, see Ben Smith, "Palin Raises $8 Million – For Obama," *Politico* blog, September 4, 2008, http://www.politico.com/blogs/bensmith/0908/Palin_raising_for_Obama_.html (accessed September 22, 2009).

[45]David Plouffe, qtd. in Wolffe, *Renegade*, p. 228.

[46]Jeff Zeleny, "Obama Camp Sets New Money Guidelines," *New York Times*, June 5, 2008, http://thecaucus.blogs.nytimes.com/2008/06/05/obama-camp-sets-new-money-guidelines/, (accessed September 22, 2009).

[47]Obama Campaign, qtd. in The Institute of Politics, John F. Kennedy School of Government at Harvard University, *Campaign for President: The Managers Look at 2008* (Lanham, MD: Rowman & Littlefield, 2009), p. 180.

[48]Adam Nagourney and Jeff Zeleny, "Obama Forgoes Public Funds in First for Major Candidate," *New York Times*, June 20, 2008, http://www.nytimes.com/2008/06/20/us/politics/20obamacnd.html (accessed September 22, 2009).

[49]David B. Magleby, "Conclusions and Implications for Future Elections," *The Other Campaign: Soft Money and Issue Advocacy in the 2000 Congressional Elections*, ed. David B. Magleby (Lanham, MD: Rowman & Littlefield, 2003), p. 229; David B. Magleby, "The Lingering Effects of a Night Spent Dancing," *Dancing Without Partners: How Candidates, Parties, and Interest Groups Interact in the Presidential Campaign*, ed. David B. Magleby, J. Quin Monson, and Kelly D. Patterson (Lanham, MD: Rowman & Littlefield, 2007), pp. 167–68.

[50]Ibid.

[51]Christopher Cooper and Laura Meckler, "Obama Takes in a Record $150 Million, But McCain Narrows Gap in Some Polls," *Wall Street Journal*, October 20, 2008, http://online.wsj.com/article/SB122441294251948009.html (accessed September 16, 2009).

[52]Bill McInturff, qtd. in The Institute of Politics, *Managers Look at 2008*, p. 183.

[53]James A. Thurber, "Dynamics and Transformation of American Campaigns," *Campaigns and Elections American Style*, 3rd ed. (Boulder, CO: Westview Press, 2009), p. 12.

[54]Andrei Scheinkman, Xaquín G.V., Alan McLean, and Stephan Weitberg, "The Ad Wars," *New York Times*, December 1, 2008, http://elections.nytimes.com/2008/president/advertising/index.html (accessed September 22, 2009).

[55]Jim Rutenberg, "Obama Infomercial, a Closing Argument to the Everyman," *New York Times*, October 8, 2008, http://www.nytimes.com/2008/10/29/us/politics/29obama.html (accessed September 22, 2009).

[56]The Institute of Politics, John F. Kennedy School of Government at Harvard University, *Campaign for President: The Managers Look at 2008* (Lanham, MD: Rowman & Littlefield, 2009), p. 113.

[57]Balz and Johnson, *Battle*, pp. 305–06.

[58]Ibid.

[59]Wolffe, *Renegade*, p. 60.

[60]Jon Carson, Obama for America national field director, interview by David Magleby, December 11, 2008.

[61]Dennis W. Johnson, "An Election Like No Other?" in *Campaigning for President 2008* (New York: Routledge, 2009), pp. 12–13.

[62]Mark Silva, "Obama's Ground Game: 770 Field Offices," *Chicago Tribune*, http://www.swamppolitics.com/news/politics/blog/2008/10/obamas_ground_game_770_field_o.html (accessed August 11, 2009).

[63]David B. Magleby, "Elections as Team Sports: Spending by Candidates, Political Parties, and Interest Groups in the 2008 Election Cycle," *The Change Election: Money, Mobilization, and Persuasion in the 2008 Federal Elections* (Provo, UT: Center for the Study of Elections and Democracy, 2009), p. 65.

[64]Wolffe, *Renegade*, p. 80.

[65]Abdon M. Pallasch, "'Ruthless' for Obama," *Chicago Sun-Times*, September 4, 2007, http://www.suntimes.com/news/elections/540781,CST-NWS-camp04.article (accessed August 7, 2009).

[66]Qtd. in Peter Dreier, "Will Obama Inspire a New Generation of Organizers?," *Dissent Magazine*, June 25, 2008, http://www.dissentmagazine.org/online.php?id=109 (accessed October 23, 2009).

[67]Peter Dreier, "Will Obama Inspire a New Generation of Organizers?" *Dissent*, Spring 2008, http://dissentmagazine.org/article/?article=1215 (accessed September 16, 2009).

[68]Wolffe, *Renegade*, p. 81.

[69]Ewen MacAskill, "Down in Des Moines Obama Revives the Ghost of JFK," *The Guardian*, December 1, 2007, http://www.guardian.co.uk/world/2007/dec/01/barackobama.uselections2008 (accessed September 2009).

[70]Dan Morain, "Campaign '08: Controversy and Money; Clinton, Obama Spend Differently; She Pays Bigger Bucks for High-end Catering and Top Aides, Whereas He Shells out More on Media and Polling," *Los Angeles Times*, February 22, 2009.

[71]Scott Helman and Sasha Issenberg, "McCain Courts Conservatives After Romney Quits Candidacy," *Boston Globe*, February 8, 2008, http://www.boston.com/news/nation/articles/2008/02/08/mccain_courts_conservatives_after_romney_quits_candidacy/ (accessed September 22, 2009).

[72]Eric Heberlig, Peter Francia, and Steven Greene, "The Conditional Party Teams of the 2008 North Carolina Federal Elections," *The Change Election: Money, Mobilization, and Persuasion in the 2008 Federal Elections* (Provo, UT: Center for the Study of Elections and Democracy, 2009), p. 109.

[73]Balz and Johnson, *Battle*, p. 101.

[74]Green, "The Amazing Money Machine."

[75]Wolffe, *Renegade*, pp. 79–80.

[76]David Trichler, Obama For America field staffer, interview by David Magleby, November 21, 2008.

[77]For an example of how this concept is applied, see Catherine Marie Shaw, *The Campaign Manager: Running and Winning Local Elections*, 3rd ed. (Boulder, Co: Westview, 2004), p. 133.

[78]Matt Bai, *The Argument: Billionaires, Bloggers, and the Battle to Remake Democratic Politics* (New York: Penguin Press, 2007), p. 25.

[79]Byron York, "America Coming Together Comes Apart," *National Review*, August 3, 2005, http://www.nationalreview.com/york/york200508030928.asp (accessed September 22, 2009).

[80]David B. Magleby, J. Quin Monson, and Kelly D. Patterson, "Introduction," *Dancing Without Partners: How Candidates, Parties, and Interest Groups Interact in the Presidential Campaign* (Lanham, MD: Rowman & Littlefield, 2007), pp.16–17.

[81]Harvard University Institute of Politics, "Study Groups Fall 2007: People, Power & Electoral Organizing in the Modern Campaign," http://www.iop.harvard.edu/Programs/Fellows-Study-Groups/Past-Study-Groups/People,-Power-Electoral-Organizing-in-the-Modern-Campaign (accessed August 14, 2009).

[82]Ken Strasma, President, Strategic Telemetry, interview by David Magleby, December 2, 2008.

[83]Mike Dorning, "Obama's 10 Percent Solution," *Chicago Tribune*, June 25, 2008, http://www.swamppolitics.com/news/politics/blog/2008/06/obamas_10_percent_solution.html (accessed September 16, 2009).

[84]Sara Murray, "New Voters Back Obama; Turnout Unsure," *Wall Street Journal*, October 29, 2008, http://online.wsj.com/article/SB122524759452778955.html (accessed September 16, 2009).

[85]Balz and Johnson, *Battle*, p. 368.

[86]Institute of Politics, John F. Kennedy School of Government at Harvard University, *Campaign for President: The Managers Look at 2008* (Lanham, MD: Rowman & Littlefield, 2009), p. 98.

[87]Joe Rospars, Obama for America new media director, interview by David Magleby, January 28, 2009.

[88]Balz and Johnson, *Battle*, p. 365.

[89]David Plouffe, qtd. in Institute of Politics, *Managers Look at 2008*, p. 204.

[90]Balz and Johnson, *Battle*, p. 368.

[91]CNN, "Exit Polls," *CNN.com*, http://www.cnn.com/ELECTION/2008/results/polls/#val=USP00p5 (accessed September 22, 2009); see also Michael McDonald and Thomas Schaller, "Voter Mobilization in the 2008 Presidential Election," *The Change Election: Money, Mobilization, and Persuasion in the 2008 Federal Elections* (Provo, UT: Center for the Study of Elections and Democracy, 2009), p. 104; see also the National Election Study for 2008, which found 24% reporting having been contacted by Republicans and 32% by Democrats. Respondents in 2000 were 3% more likely to have been contacted by Republicans, but in 2004 were 3% more likely to have been contacted by Democrats. On average since 1956 only 1% separates the two parties in the proportion of the public reporting having been contacted by them in federal general elections; The American National Election Studies (www.electionstudies.org). The 1948–2004 ANES Cumulative Data File. Stanford University and the University of Michigan [producers and distributors], 2005; The American National Election Studies (ANES; www.electionstudies.org). The ANES 2008 Time Series Study, Stanford University and the University of Michigan, 2008.

[92]Joe Trippi, John Edwards's '08 senior advisor, interview by David Magleby, December 18, 2008.

Chapter 3

The Presidential Media Environment in the Age of Obama

Martin P. Wattenberg

If the power of the presidency is the power to persuade, then the ability to communicate with the American public is one key tool in exercising that power. When presidents address the nation, they expect to have a large viewing audience, and that their message will continue to permeate the public consciousness through news reports for days afterwards. But a series of changes in the mass media environment have made it much less likely that these expectations will be fulfilled today, compared to just several decades ago. A tale of the initial speeches given to Congress by President Ronald Reagan in 1981 and President Barack Obama in 2009 provides a good illustration of the profound changes in the presidential media environment discussed in this chapter.

President Reagan addressed Congress during prime time on February 18, 1981, to outline his proposed policies for economic recovery. Reagan's speech was covered live on CBS, NBC, and ABC and garnered a Nielsen rating of 60.0, meaning that three-fifths of the American public watched it. According to Matthew Baum and Samuel Kernell, such massive audiences were not unusual for presidential addresses in the broadcasting era, when these three networks controlled an overwhelming share of the viewing audience.[1] Furthermore, Reagan's ability to communicate his message extended beyond the enormous size of his live television audience—he could also expect most people to be reading and viewing news reports about his remarks soon afterwards. The next day, at least 55 percent of the public could be expected to pick up a newspaper containing stories about the president's speech, as surveys at that time found this percentage of survey participants read a newspaper every day. Later that evening, roughly 38 percent could be expected to view some coverage of the president's speech on the highly rated national TV newscasts at dinnertime.

The situation was markedly different when President Obama went to Capitol Hill on February 24, 2009 to set forth his proposals for dealing with the economic crisis. In addition to CBS, NBC, and ABC, Obama's speech was also telecast by FOX, FOX News, CNN, MSNBC, CNBC, Telemundo, and Univision. Yet, whereas Reagan received an audience rating of 60.0 from his appearance on three networks, Obama achieved a combined rating of just 32.5 on 10 channels. In this age of narrowcasting, in which a plethora of channels appeal to specialized audiences, large audiences are increasingly rare—and even presidents usually do not achieve them. Not only was the audience rating for Obama's speech about half of Reagan's, but he also could not count on a regular audience of news consumers learning about his remarks the next day. Whereas 55 percent of the public read a newspaper every day in the early 1980s, by the time Obama assumed office only about 32 percent did so. And the typical ratings of the nightly newscasts on the three traditional broadcast networks had plummeted from 38 to just 16. (Of course, there are now also cable news shows available to most viewers. But even taking into account these shows—which typically get ratings of less than two—would scarcely make up for the lost audience of the network broadcasts.)

The diminishing size of the audience for presidential messages, as well as for national news, means that President Obama faces a significantly more difficult task in getting messages through to the entire public than at any time since the birth of mass media. In addition, the nature of the audience no longer befits the ideal notion of a nationally elected officer who is president of *all* the people. The audience for politics is now highly skewed in terms of age, with young adults being less likely to follow what the president is doing. Such a bias may not seem too serious because everyone eventually gets older. But it is a bias that degrades representation, as young people do clearly have interests and policy priorities that are distinct from their elders. It is also a particularly vexing problem for President Obama because the very group of young Americans who helped elect him are going to be the most difficult for him to get his message to as president.

THE DECLINING AUDIENCE FOR PRESIDENTIAL SPEECHES

Like most regularly occurring live events shown on television, presidential speeches have seen their average rating drop by at least 40 percent compared to the 1970s and early 1980s. As displayed in Table 1, presidential State of the Union speeches are in good company in experiencing declining ratings with other major live events, such as baseball's World Series and All-Star game, the NCAA basketball finals, the Miss Universe Pageant, and the awards ceremonies for the Grammys and Oscars. Only the Super Bowl has not seen its ratings decline substantially, as "Super Bowl Sunday" has become a secular religious festival for many Americans, with the crime rate being reduced more during the game than probably any other time than Christmas Day.

Table 1. TV Ratings of Major Prime-Time Yearly Events, 1970–2009

	1970 -74	1975 -79	1980 -84	1985 -89	1990 -94	1995 -99	2000 -04	2005 -09	Decline from peak
State of the Union	—	49.6	50.4	37.5	37.5	31.1	30.1	27.8	-45%
World Series	27.9	29.5	27.4	23.6	20.6	16.7	13.7	10.1	-66%
MLB All-Star	25.1	24.7	22.7	19.5	16.0	12.8	9.8	8.8	-65%
Super Bowl	41.6	44.7	47.0	45.2	42.4	43.1	41.2	42.1	-10%
NCAA BB final	—	21.0	20.8	20.7	21.0	18.3	13.7	12.3	-41%
Miss Universe Pageant	—	22.8	23.6	16.5	11.2	8.3	7.0	5.2	-78%
Grammy Awards	—	22.0	23.1	19.9	18.0	14.7	15.3	11.2	-52%
Academy Awards	39.0	34.5	33.3	28.3	29.7	30.7	25.4	22.3	-43%

Source: Nielsen Media Research.

The reason that most big events have seen their TV ratings decline is readily apparent—the fractionalization of the viewing audience that has occurred as the number of available channels has risen dramatically with the spread of cable and satellite television. At the outset of Reagan's presidency, for example, the three major networks accounted for 85 percent of the prime-time audience. Even with the addition of a fourth major network (FOX), in 2009 the comparable network share was just 40 percent. When President Reagan went on TV to give a speech or hold a press conference, many viewers had little other choice but to watch him if they had their TV on at that time. Today, not only do the major networks control substantially less of the audience, but there are numerous alternatives available, what with the typical viewer having an average of 131 channels from which to choose. One important result of this change in the television world is that the notion of a "captive audience" is a concept that no longer applies today.

The impact on President Obama's ability to reach large audiences can be seen in Table 2, which compares Nielsen ratings of prime-time presidential TV appearances during the first year of the Reagan, Clinton, and Obama administrations. All three presidents entered office committed to dealing with economic downturns, and all made at least four prime-time appearances to try to promote their domestic agendas to the Congress and the American people.

Each president saw their highest TV ratings in their second appearance, which in each case was a State of the Union address to Congress. And each president saw their ratings fall off substantially as their first year proceeded, as the novelty of watching a new president wore off. But whereas Reagan's five appearances averaged an audience of about 48 percent of the public, and Clinton's garnered an average of 36 percent, Obama's typical audience was just 24 percent. Indeed, not even Obama's most viewed early TV appearance got a rating even equal to the average enjoyed by either Reagan or Clinton in their first year.

Table 2. Nielsen Ratings for Prime-Time Televised Speeches and Press Conferences in the First Year of the Obama, Clinton, and Reagan Administrations

	Date	Rating	Event
Reagan	2/05/81	55.7	Oval office speech
Reagan	2/18/81	60.0	Congressional speech
Reagan	4/28/81	45.5	Congressional speech
Reagan	7/27/81	32.5	Oval office speech
Reagan	9/24/81	45.7	Oval office speech
Clinton	2/15/93	42.1	Oval office speech
Clinton	2/17/93	44.3	Congressional speech
Clinton	8/03/93	24.4	Oval office speech
Clinton	9/22/93	32.8	Congressional speech
Obama	2/09/09	30.8	First press conference
Obama	2/24/09	32.5	Congressional speech
Obama	3/24/09	25.9	Second press conference
Obama	4/29/09	18.8	Third press conference
Obama	7/22/09	16.3	Fourth press conference
Obama	9/09/09	19.8	Congressional speech

Source: Nielsen Media Research.

THE GENERATION GAP IN WATCHING POLITICS

The shift from broadcasting to narrowcasting has dramatically altered the amount of political exposure young adults receive while growing up, compared to that of their parents and grandparents. Because of the narrowcasting revolution—i.e., the proliferation of channels—today's young adults grew up in an environment in which the activities of the president were not as ever-present as in the recent past. It has become particularly difficult to convince a generation that has channel-surfed all their lives that they ought to tune in to what the president has to say. Presidential pronouncements and campaigns were once shared national experiences. However, the current generation of young adults is the first to grow up in a media environment in which there are few such shared experiences. Young people have therefore never known a time when most citizens paid attention to major political events. Thus, the influx of a new generation of citizens who pay much less attention to politics than their elders probably accounts for much of why President Obama's broadcast appearances have drawn a smaller percentage of the population than Clinton's or Reagan's.

Indeed, despite frequent talk of 2008 being the so-called "Year of the Youth Vote," there was much evidence throughout the campaign that young Americans were the least attuned to the year's major political events. Most notably, this all-too-familiar pattern was quite evident in Nielsen Media Research's analysis of who actually watched the political party conventions and the first two presidential debates in 2008. As can be seen in Figure 1, the results from Nielsen's people-meter sample of the viewing public,[2] reveal that the likelihood of watching one of these events was roughly proportional to one's age. In other words, people who were 40 years of age were about twice as likely to tune in to these big political events as 20-year-olds, and people who were 60 years old had viewing rates three times that of college-age adults. As I have documented extensively in my book, *Is Voting for Young People?*, although such an age pattern in viewing is common these days it was not the case back when three networks dominated the television market.[3]

In sum, the audience for politics is now one that is unrepresentative of the general adult public in terms of age. Governing in the narrowcasting age, President Obama should expect that when he uses the mass media to ostensibly address the nation he is likely to reach a much larger percentage of older citizens than younger. Given that Obama's support is concentrated amongst younger voters, this represents a major problem for him. He really needs the attention of young adults to gather support for programs like health care reform, but this group is the least likely to be tuning in to a nationally televised presidential appearance.

Figure 1. Percent Watching Some of the
Major 2008 Campaign Events by Age Group

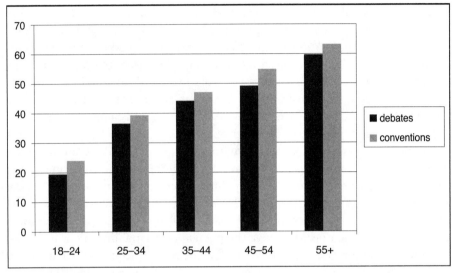

Source: Nielsen Media Research.

THE GENERATION GAP IN WATCHING TV NEWS

Of course, presidential rhetoric has a political life, and it continues long after the initial statement. The impact of what a president says rests in large part on how it is received and interpreted by the media in the days following. As President Obama wrote in his book, *The Audacity of Hope,* "I—like every politician at the federal level—am almost entirely dependent on the media to reach my constituents. It is the filter through which my votes are interpreted, my statements analyzed, my beliefs examined. For the broad public at least, I am who the media says I am."[4] In particular, when people say they've seen a presidential speech, it often merely means they have seen a sound bite or two from it on TV news. In most cases, a nationally televised presidential appearance will be reviewed and analyzed on the various news shows during the following 24 hours. Thus, the people who are currently most likely to watch TV news are probably learning the most about the president's message.

For a time, the anchors of the three nightly news broadcasts were major figures in American political life who could count on attracting large broad-based audiences night after night. As Jeff Alan writes, "For all of us who grew up with the evening news anchors in our living rooms and family rooms five nights a week, it's fair to say that we saw more of the anchors than we saw of most of our neighbors, and even some of our close friends and relatives."[5] Over the last three decades, however, the NBC, CBS, and ABC nightly news broadcasts have gone from being instrumental in setting the nation's agenda to the TV equivalent of dinosaurs on their last legs. It doesn't take too much analytical ability these days to recognize that the network news broadcasts are barely hanging on by relying on older viewers who got into the habit of viewing these shows decades ago. Just as the many beer and snack advertisements aired during a pro football game indicate the type of person most likely to be watching, the abundance of ads for ailments of the aging tells us the demographic of the network news audience."

"OK, BUT CAN HE HELP US FIND A YOUNGER AUDIENCE?"

Indeed, the data displayed in the right-hand column of Table 3 indicate that each of the nightly network newscasts now attracts an audience with a median age of 61. Only syndicated game shows like *Wheel of Fortune* and *The Price is Right* attract an older audience. Not having developed the habit of watching the nightly news, while growing up in an era of multiple entertainment options, young viewers have bypassed news programs for shows like *The Simpsons* and *Gossip Girl*.

Table 3. Median age of viewers of various TV channels and shows, 2007–2008 season (October–May)

TV CHANNELS		TV SHOWS	
FOX News	65	Wheel of Fortune	64
CNN	60	Jeopardy	63
Headline News	57	Price is Right	63
MSNBC	55	ABC Evening News	61
CBS	53	CBS Evening News	61
ABC	49	NBC Evening News	61
Travel	49	60 Minutes	60
History	49	Dancing with the Stars	55
NBC	48	Oprah	54
A&E	46	CSI	53
FOX	43	Saturday Night Live	44
ESPN	43	American Idol	42
Discovery	38	The Office	35
E!	34	Friday Night Smackdown	34
Comedy	30	America's Next Top Model	31
VH1	27	Beauty & the Geek	31
MTV	23	The Simpsons	31
Nick-at-Nite	18	Gossip Girl	27
Nikelodeon	11	George Lopez	25

Source: Steve Sternberg, "The Median Age Report," Media Insights, June 30, 2008. http://tvbythenumbers.com/wp-content/uploads/2008/06/2008-median-age-report.pdf.

Of course, today's viewers also have alternatives to the 30-minute network news shows in the form of round-the-clock news on CNN, MSNBC, and Fox News Channel. On the positive side, there can be little doubt that there is a good deal of *potential* for learning about politics from watching a substantial amount of political coverage on the cable news networks. However, as many critics of these channels have said, there is reason to be skeptical about how much people can actually learn from the free-flowing spirited discussions that often dominate these channels. For example, President Obama says he doesn't watch the cable news channels, because "it feels like WWF wrestling." Softening this derogatory remark, the president went on to say that "It's not even necessarily that there's not good reporting on it; it's just that everyone is having to accelerate to get the next story, the new story, and if there's a story that people think is going to sell, then they overdo it."[6]

Cable news may well be different in terms of content and format than the traditional network news, but the age distribution of its audience is virtually the same. As displayed in the left-hand column of Table 3, the median age of prime-time viewers (8:00–11:00 p.m.) of the four major cable news channels ranges between 55 and 65. The differences between the cable channels can probably be accounted for by the partisan bias in their respective audiences. Because Republicans are much more likely to watch FOX News than Democrats, and because Republicans draw their strongest support these days from older voters, the audience for FOX News is clearly the oldest. And on the other side of the fence, MSNBC's appeal to Democrats provides them with an audience that is not quite so old. Yet, compared to other channels that focus on specific forms of entertainment, even MSNBC's audience is unusually old. Young people clearly prefer to watch channels like Nick at Nite, MTV, VH1, Comedy Central, and E!, as opposed to news channels.

THE GENERATION GAP IN READING NEWSPAPERS

If one really wants to be well informed about political matters, reading a newspaper regularly is one of the very best ways to gather detailed information about current affairs. Thus, when President George W. Bush told a FOX News reporter that he didn't read newspapers, many pundits and scholars gasped. Longtime White House correspondent Helen Thomas wrote a widely cited critical piece about this revelation entitled "No Wonder Bush Doesn't Connect With the Country." In this piece, Thomas argued that: "Anyone who wants to stay in touch with national, international and local events looks forward to reading the newspaper every day. The variety and breadth of newspaper stories make Americans the best-informed people in the world."[7] Of course, President Bush maintained that he did not need to read newspapers because his chief of staff and national security advisor briefed him on the news every day. But this satisfied few critics, who wondered whether even the most trusted aides could be expected to relay a full report of the news of the day to the commander-in-chief.

Left unsaid in this hullabaloo was the hard fact that the percentage of the American public that reads a daily newspaper has been declining for quite some time, a trend that has been driven by generational replacement. Whether

Bush's avoidance of newspapers was a good practice for a president or not, the fact that so many Americans no longer make a habit of reading a daily newspaper made it easier for a president to say he doesn't either. (Since Obama took over the presidency, however, it should be noted that he has said that he reads several newspapers a day).[8]

Table 4. Cohort analysis of percent reading the newspaper every day

	2008	1993	1978
Born in:			
1980s	15	—	—
1970s	21	22	—
1960s	27	28	—
1950s	36	40	37
1940s	49	58	48
1930s	62	59	67
1920s	76	72	68
1910s	—	72	81

Source: General Social Surveys for 1978, 1993, and 2008.

The generational nature of this trend is demonstrated in Table 4, which compares the age patterns of newspaper readership at three points in time: 1978, 1993, and 2008. In each year, one can clearly see that the likelihood of being a regular newspaper reader increases with age. Notably, this age gap has widened over time as each new age cohort has set new low marks for newspaper readership. For example, only 15 percent of Americans born in the 1980s said they read a newspaper every day in 2008. As these young people are gradually replacing a generation that had been five times as likely to be in the daily habit of reading a newspaper, it is no wonder that virtually all U.S. newspapers are experiencing serious declines in their circulation. Of course, there is the theoretical possibility that as today's young adults age they will get more into the newspaper habit. However, looking across the rows of Table 4, one can see that in the past, age groups have been remarkably consistent from decade to decade in their newspaper reading frequency, as these habits are apparently well established by early adulthood.

Given this generational trend, the financial viability of a printed newspaper delivered to your front door every morning is currently on very shaky ground. Long-established newspapers in Denver and Seattle went out of business early in Obama's first year, and papers in Philadelphia, Chicago, Los Angeles, Minneapolis, and Baltimore, amongst others, have filed for Chapter 11 bankruptcy. The Newspaper Association of America reported that the total advertising revenues that newspapers took in during the second quarter of 2009 was $6,817 million, as compared with $11,311 million in the second quarter of 2007.[9] With such a precipitous decline in revenues, many newspapers are currently struggling to survive.

Many people believe the future of the newspaper business lies with the Internet, and most major newspapers are currently making some money via advertising revenue from their online editions. However, Internet revenues for newspapers have fallen far short of what is needed to maintain a full staff of reporters and editors. As of mid-2009, ad revenues from the Internet represented only about 10 percent of newspapers' total take from advertising.[10] Furthermore, amongst the papers that have tried charging a fee for access to their reporting, only those that focus on business news, such as the *Wall Street Journal* and the *Financial Times*, have proved successful in selling paid Internet subscriptions. Thus, when media mogul

Rupert Murdoch said in August 2009 that his newspapers would soon be charging for content on the Internet, his remarks were met with a good deal of skepticism. For example, media critic Howard Kurtz wrote in the *Washington Post* that "in a world of Twitter feeds and gigabytes of gossip and a thousand other distractions, most people will see no need to pay for news. There will always be enough aggregators out there for them to cherry-pick the latest headlines, photos and video."[11] In short, the prospects for the newspaper business in the age of Obama are much like that of General Motors and Chrysler. Newspapers may well survive, but, if so, it will likely be in a much slimmed-down version of their former prominence in American life.

THE STILL UNFULFILLED PROMISE OF THE INTERNET

Some scholars have expressed quite optimistic predictions that the development of the Internet will be a boon for American democracy. As any college student knows, the Internet is the ultimate research tool. Yet, simply because so much political information is at one's fingertips via the Internet doesn't necessarily mean that many people will take advantage of these unprecedented opportunities to become well informed. One of the things that makes the Internet different from TV is that is always purposive—that is, what people see is exclusively the product of their own intentional choices. Politics is only one of a myriad of subjects that one can find out about on the Internet. Most Americans have a fairly limited interest in politics, and therefore will not often be motivated to use the Internet to look up detailed information about politics.

In the 2008 National Election Study, a nation-wide sample was asked before the election how often in a typical week they reviewed news on the Internet. Overall, just 33 percent said they did so five days a week or more, thereby making them regular consumers of Internet news. Narrowing the focus to campaign news in the postelection interviews, this study found that only 13 percent of the public said they read, watched, or listened to information on the Internet about the presidential campaign "a good many times." Contrary to any notion that young adults make up for their relative lack of consumption of traditional news sources by getting news from the Internet, these percentages were exactly the same among respondents under the age of 30. In sum, young adults in the "Age of Obama" can potentially learn a tremendous amount about politics from the Internet, if they so choose, but it would appear that relatively few are choosing to do so.

INFOTAINMENT AND POLITICS: CAN ENTERTAINMENT SHOWS REALLY INFORM PEOPLE ABOUT POLITICS?

One way of learning about politics that does draw a notably young audience is the so-called "infotainment" genre, like *The Daily Show with Jon Stewart* and *The Colbert Report*. A series of Pew Research Center surveys during the last two presidential campaigns have found that a substantial percentage of young people say that these shows are one of their top sources for learning about politics. Commenting on this survey finding, Jon Stewart at first dismissed out of hand any notion that young people were turning to his comedy show to learn about political events. Later on, though, his show adopted the slogan of "Keeping America Informed—Unintentionally." Such a catchphrase astutely captures how comedy shows can make a marginal contribution to their viewers' store of political information.

As Stewart has pointed out on numerous occasions, the goal of his show is to entertain people, not inform them. Thus, the choice of topics for the show is necessarily focused on whatever story angles can best provide fodder for amusing spoofs. A tragedy like the mass shootings at Virginia Tech in 2007 dominated the news broadcasts for a week but wasn't mentioned on the comedy shows, as such shows won't touch upon tragedies. Nor will complex policy issues usually be covered, as too few viewers would likely get the punch-lines without the necessary detailed background information, which the show's writers wouldn't want to review. On the other hand, a story about a governor becoming embroiled in a sex scandal (e.g., Elliot Spitzer of New York, or Mark Sanford of South Carolina) will be treated like a gift from heaven to infotainment shows. Indeed, David Niven et al.'s scholarly analysis of the political content of comedy shows found that they rarely included issue content, instead highlighting the miscues of politicians.[12] As Matthew Baum explains, "by focusing on candidates' personal qualities rather than 'arcane' policy debates," such shows "can appeal to their relatively apolitical, entertainment-seeking audiences."[13]

Nevertheless, scholars have found that by wrapping bits of political content into an amusing package, infotainment makes politics more appealing to viewers who might otherwise ignore the subject, and thereby adds to the political knowledge of some. For example, Paul Brewer and Xiaoxia Cao found that seeing a candidate on programs like *The Daily Show* or *The Tonight Show* was positively related to knowledge about the 2004 primary campaign, even after controlling for many well-known influences on political information.[14] Barry Hollander specifically examined what young adults take away from infotainment shows, and concluded that that they glean "at least modest amounts of campaign information from such content."[15] And Baum found that exposure to entertainment-oriented TV talk shows among voters with lower-than-average political interest had a significant impact on how they evaluated the candidates and whom they voted for.[16]

Although infotainment shows are making a difference in politics today, several academic studies have revealed their limitations in terms of actually helping viewers understand the political world. Hollander's in-depth analysis of what young people learn from political comedy found that exposure to such television shows was mostly associated with simple recognition of campaign events, as opposed to recall of specific pieces of knowledge. In other words, whatever learning occurred was on a fairly superficial level. Such a conclusion has been further bolstered by Young Mie Kim and John Vishak's experimental study, which compared learning from traditional news programs to infotainment coverage of the same political events. They found that subjects who were shown Jon Stewart's coverage of the Supreme Court nomination process, then in progress, learned less factual information than those who were shown a similar amount of coverage of this topic culled from the nightly news. The title of their article—"Just Laugh! You Don't Need to Remember"—nicely summarizes their most important finding with regard to infotainment shows.[17] Finally, a recent study of how young adults react to *The Colbert Report* provides especially compelling evidence of how political messages can be obscured amidst laughter. Jody Baumgartner and Jonathan Morris found that young people who were shown some of Stephen Colbert's ridicule of conservative media figures like Bill O'Reilly actually became more supportive of Republicans and their policies. Colbert's criticism of conservatives is indirect, performed through what knowledgeable observers would consider to be not-so-subtle mockery. However, for casual viewers, the right-wing arguments Colbert exaggerates apparently get through much better than the absurd aspect of his portrayal. As Baumgartner and Morris theorize, "the humor may block, disrupt, or distract" processing of the central political message "by increasing the likeability or trustworthiness of the source (Colbert)."[18]

Ironically, it is the fact that infotainment shows are not designed to convey political information that attracts politicians to make personal appearances on them. As the old saying goes, "If you want to go duck hunting, you need to go where the ducks are." And in the era of narrowcasting, wherein the inadvertent audience scarcely exists, people who are not much interested in politics can only be reached by appearing on shows that don't normally do politics. In explaining why politicians hit the talk show circuit, Baum writes, "If America's political leaders wish to communicate with members of the public who are not predisposed to seek out political information, they must put the information where these potential voters are likely to notice it. In part, this involves tailoring messages to the sensibilities of E-talk show audiences."[19]

CONCLUSION

Not everyone agrees that politicians, particularly the president, should take advantage of so many opportunities to be on various TV shows. Indeed, political commentator and staunch Obama supporter Bill Maher made a news splash in June 2009 when he chastised President Obama for devoting so much time and effort to being on TV. Maher snickered that, "It's getting to where you can't turn on your TV without seeing Obama. . . . Come on, sir, you don't have to be on television every minute of every day. You're the president, not a rerun of *Law and Order*." Comparing Obama to Lindsay Lohan, of all people, Maher bemoaned that he didn't want the president to be a TV star "because TV stars are too worried about being popular—and too concerned with getting renewed."[20] Maher's critique drew attention not just for its wit, but also due to the fact that he tapped into what a number of observers were thinking at the time. Indeed, President Obama's press secretary, Robert Gibbs, was eventually compelled to respond to the charge that the president had been overexposed in the media. As Gibbs explained, "The way the media is structured these days and the fact that it is so segmented and split up means that in order to get something to go through, you've got to do multiple platforms."[21]

In light of the data reviewed in this chapter, Gibbs's explanation makes a great deal of sense. To someone like Bill Maher, who monitors what President Obama is doing day in and day out, it is easy to see how the impression could be formed that the president is obsessed with being on TV whenever he can. But due to the fragmentation of the audience over recent decades, what Obama is in fact doing is appealing to a few million people in one venue, a couple million in a totally different one, etc. Unlike President Reagan, and others before him, Obama cannot count on just giving one big speech that will be watched by roughly half of the population, and then related indirectly to even more people via widely viewed news programs and newspapers with large circulations.

The fragmentation of the audience for politics over the past several decades has had numerous consequences for the American presidency. In some sense, the presidency is a less powerful position than it used to be, as presidents have lost the ability to communicate their messages to a broad cross section of the American public anytime they see fit. This power to communicate directly with the American public was long thought to be an invaluable asset. As Fred Friendly of CBS wrote in 1973, "No mighty King, no ambitious Emperor, no Pope, no prophet ever dreamt of such an awesome pulpit, such a magic wand."[22] As the media environment has fractionalized, President Obama finds himself with a pulpit that is not nearly so awesome. Like President Reagan before him, President Obama is frequently called "the Great Communicator." However, the opportunities to use the bully pulpit of the presidency have been sharply reduced during the intervening years between the Reagan and Obama administrations.

On the other hand, the positive news for President Obama is that, compared to presidents several decades ago, he is likely to face less competition from the media in setting the agenda. Declining audiences for the nightly network news have made it far more difficult for these outlets to shape the national agenda in the way they did decades ago.[23] Such a change does not necessarily mean that a president will be able to successfully direct the nation's agenda, but at least TV news no longer presents a potentially powerful obstacle.

The fragmentation of the news audience has also made the job of targeting presidential messages to the attentive public somewhat easier. In particular, presidents who can tailor their policies to please the over-65 age group stand to be in much better shape than those who fail to do so, as seniors are currently the group most attentive to political news." Although it would be hard to argue that the age bias in presidential audiences is a positive develop-ment for representative democracy, it is unfortunately always easier to please some of the people than all of the people.

For President Obama, however, reaching his youthful core of supporters is going to be difficult in the present media environment, for they are by far the least likely to be paying attention to traditional sources of TV news and newspapers. In theory, the Internet might provide Obama with a means for reaching out to young people. But given the incredible variety of options one has when browsing the Internet, it is questionable whether many young adults will pay attention to politics aside from during the heat of an election campaign. If Obama can succeed in reaching out to these young people via the Internet, his administration will truly be revolutionary in terms of politi-cal communication.

QUESTIONS TO CONSIDER

1. Do you think that President Obama can successfully use the Internet to get his message out to most young adults? Among the young people you know, are many likely to watch Obama's video presentations, which are now regularly posted on the Internet, and/or to subscribe to the e-mails the White House sends out? Why or why not?
2. Do you think people can learn much about politics from entertainment shows like *The Daily Show with Jon Stewart*? Should President Obama make an effort to appear on shows like this?
3. Based on the information provided in this chapter, was it really easier for President Reagan to set the public agenda than President Obama? Why or why not?

NOTES

[1]Matthew A. Baum and Samuel Kernell, "Has Cable Ended the Golden Age of Presidential Television?," *American Political Science Review*, March 1999, pp. 99–114.

[2]For a good discussion of the methodological advantages of Nielsen's people meter data as opposed to self-reports in survey data, see Markus Prior, "The Immensely Inflated News Audience: Assessing Bias in Self-Reported News Exposure," *Public Opinion Quarterly*, Spring 2009, pp. 130–43.

[3]See Martin P. Wattenberg, *Is Voting for Young People?* (New York: Longman, 2008), chap. 3.

[4]Barack Obama, *The Audacity of Hope*, (New York: Three Rivers Press, 2006), p. 121.

[5]Jeff Alan, *Anchoring America: The Changing Face of Network News* (Chicago: Bonus Books, 2003), p. xiii.

[6]NBC News, "A Day in the Life of Obama's White House," June 3, 2009, http://www.msnbc.msn.com/id/31050780/ (date accessed: October 24, 2009).

[7]See Helen Thomas, "No Wonder Bush Doesn't Connect With the Rest of the Country," *Seattle Post-Intelligencer*, October 15, 2003, http://www.seattlepi.com/opinion/143851_thomas15.html (date accessed: October 24, 2009).

[8]One can even find a photo of Obama reading a newspaper at the White House's official Flickr site. See http://www.flickr.com/photos/whitehouse/3484018149/ (date accessed: October 24, 2009).

[9]See http://www.naa.org/TrendsandNumbers/Advertising-Expenditures.aspx (date accessed: October 24, 2009).

[10]Ibid.

[11]Howard Kurtz, "The Press Loves a Hero, but . . . Presidential Commission Won't Save Newspapers," *Washington Post*, August 17, 2009, http://www.washingtonpost.com/wp-dyn/content/article/2009/08/16/AR2009081601529.html (date accessed: October 24, 2009).

[12]David Niven, S. Robert Lichter, and Daniel Amundson, "The Political Content of Late Night Comedy," *Harvard International Journal of Press/Politics*, March 2003, pp. 118–33.

[13]Matthew A. Baum, "Talking the Vote: Why Presidential Candidates Hit the Talk Show Circuit," *American Journal of Political Science*, April 2005, p. 214.

[14]Paul R. Brewer and Xiaoxia Cao, "Candidate Appearances on Soft News Shows and Public Knowledge About Primary Campaigns," *Journal of Broadcasting & Electronic Media*, March 2006, p. 18–35.

[15]Barry A. Hollander, "Late-Night Learning: Do Entertainment Programs Increase Political Campaign Knowledge for Young Viewers?," *Journal of Broadcasting and Electronic Media*, December 2005, p. 412.

[16]Baum, "Talking the Vote."

[17]Young Mie Kim and John Vishak, "Just Laugh! You Don't Need to Remember: The Effects of Entertainment Media on Political Information Acquisition and Information Processing in Political Judgment," *Journal of Communication*, June 2008, p. 338–60.

[18]Jody C. Baumgartner and Jonathan S. Morris, "One 'Nation,' Under Stephen? The Effects of *The Colbert Report* on American Youth," *Journal of Broadcasting and Electronic Media*, December 2008, p. 635.

[19]Baum, "Talking the Vote," p. 230.

[20]Bill Maher, "Enough with the Obamathon," *Los Angeles Times*, June 12, 2009. The video clip of Maher saying much the same thing on his TV program can be seen at http://www.youtube.com/watch?v=ewmruk69SIo (date accessed: October 24, 2009).

[21]Peter Baker, "Obama Complains About the News Cycle but Manipulates It, Worrying Some," *New York Times*, July 23, 2009, http://www.nytimes.com/2009/07/24/us/politics/24memo.html (date accessed: October 24, 2009).

[22]Fred W. Friendly, "Foreword," In Newton Minow et al., *Presidential Television* (New York: Basic Books, 1973), p. vii.

[23]For a classic investigation of how network news shaped the agenda in the Cronkite era, see Shanto Iyengar and Donald R. Kinder, *News that Matters Television and American Public Opinion* (Chicago: University of Chicago Press, 1987).

Chapter 4

Obama and the Federal Bureaucracy

Paul C. Light

Barack Obama took immediate control of the vast federal bureaucracy following the 2008 election. He moved quickly to name his White House staff, announced his choices for department heads only weeks before the holidays, and began reviewing every federal department and agency, looking for ways to improve performance and save money. He even created a new White House performance office to jettison government programs that do not work. By Inauguration Day, he had clearly established himself as the government's administrator-in-chief.

Most of Obama's initial success was rooted in his decision to begin planning for the transition to the presidency even before he won the election. Although Obama announced his planning effort in early July of 2000, he actually began well before the first Democratic presidential primary, six months earlier. He appointed the head of the Center for American Process, a liberal think tank, to lead the preparation, and put former Clinton administration Chief of Staff John Podesta in charge.

The planning staff started work by sorting the major issues the new president would face. They divided the agenda into at least three dozen areas—from solving the economic crisis to health care reform, ending the Iraq War, controlling nuclear weapons, reversing global warming, allowing stem cell research, trimming Social Security, repairing civil rights, and restoring public confidence in the presidency.

The list showed just how ambitious Obama intended to be. Within days of his inauguration on January 20, 2001, Obama had embraced the largest agenda in recent presidential history. Within several weeks, he had convinced Congress to pass a $787 billion package to stimulate the economy and had signed the Serve America Act, which expanded opportunities for volunteering for young and older Americans alike. Within months, he began developing a new health care package, was pushing forward on global warming legislation, and had created dozens of new White House positions to oversee his rapidly growing agenda.

TAKING CONTROL OF THE BUREAUCRACY

Obama used specific strategies to take control of government, even before his inauguration. To date, these strategies have given him strong controls of the

2.7 million civil servants who work for the federal government and U.S. Postal Service. As commander-in-chief, he is also clearly in charge of the 1.4 million men and women who serve in the military.

Obama took five steps to take early control of the bureaucracy: (1) appoint the White House staff, (2) fill the top political jobs in the bureaucracy, (3) assess the performance of the bureaucracy in search of key trouble spots, (4) make government service "cool" again, as he promised in his campaign, and (5) decide how to make decisions on the big issues on his ambitious agenda.

The White House Staff

Obama's first step toward gaining control of the bureaucracy involved the White House staff. He was faster than any recent president in appointing the 40 top members of the staff, defining their roles, and augmenting his power by appointing half a dozen senior aides to coordinate decisions on the major issues on his agenda.

These "czars," as they are called, work in the White House and manage the complex process of building Obama's legislative proposals on global warming, the economy, urban policy, health care reform, cybersecurity, information technology, and economic renewal. Obama also gave significant responsibilities for managing the $787 economic stimulus package to Vice President Joseph Biden. In all of these cases, the czars and vice president have the authority to draft and administer legislation that would have come directly from the departments and agencies in previous administrations.

Obama's most important White House appointment was his chief of staff, former Illinois Congressman Rahm Emanuel. Emanuel has a well-deserved reputation for making tough decisions, disciplining the staff, and making sure that the president has access to all of the information needed to make decisions. Emanuel has been involved in every major decision the president has made, including the nomination of Sonia Sotomayor as the first Latina Supreme Court Justice, to Obama's speech to the Muslim world promising a new era of peace.

Obama also appointed experienced Washington insiders to other key posts in the White House, including press secretary, the chief White House lawyer, the head of the National Security Council, the director of the Office of Management and Budget, and the domestic policy staff. Because so many of these staffers had attended prestigious universities such as Harvard, Yale, and Stanford, and were lawyers or former college professors, Obama was soon under fire for creating what some critics called the most elitist White House staff in history.

But Obama also appointed many younger members of his campaign staff who had been intimately involved in using new technologies to boost his candidacy for president in 2007 and 2008. Many of these younger aides had not attended elite universities. One of his top aides graduated from the University of Montana, another from North Carolina State, and another from the State University of New York at Geneseo. And most came into office without law degrees and doctorates. They created an important counterbalance to the more elitist tone of the White House, and even created a bit of generation gap in the White House between staffers who were older than Obama versus those were younger than Obama. As Table 1 shows, the White House is distinctly diverse.

Table 1: The Changing Face of the White House Staff

Characteristic	Total White House Staff	Younger Aides	Older Aides
Degrees from prestige universities	50%	80%	39%
Women	44%	40%	48%
Nonwhite	33%	27%	38%

Source: Paul C. Light, "Not So Elite After All," *Washington Post*, December 12, 2008.

Filling the Top Jobs in the Bureaucracy

Obama's second strategy for taking control of the bureaucracy involved the appointment of his department and agency heads. Obama scored well in making his initial appointments, moving faster than any president in recent history. But he make several mistakes that led to the early withdrawals of former Senate Majority Leader Tom Daschle as secretary of Health and Human Services, New Mexico Governor Bill Richardson as secretary of the Department of Commerce, and several lower-level aides.

Although he moved very quickly in appointing his White House staff, he was soon bogged down in the notoriously slow presidential appointments process. Whereas White House staffers serve at the pleasure of the president, meaning they can be hired and fired by the president alone, Obama also had to select nearly 500 people who are subject to Senate confirmation. The process for appointing these very visible positions is much more difficult because the Senate is slow, the potential risks of a bad appointment are high, and the public and media scrutiny of each nominee's record is so intense.

There is no question that the appointments process is broken. The process itself imposes one delay after another, steadily increasing the amount of time needed to bring a new administration into office. Whereas the Kennedy administration was up and running within three months of Inauguration Day, the second Bush administration waited more than eight months on average to complete its long list of cabinet and subcabinet appointments. The delays have raised the importance of the de facto subcabinet composed of appointees who serve solely at the pleasure of the president without Senate confirmation.

According to a random sample survey of Reagan–Clinton appointees, this appointments process has become the most significant barrier to service. Delays are common, even among highly qualified appointees, and complaints about the Senate and White House are high. Former appointees report that neither institution acts responsibly in fulfilling their constitutional duties to fill the top jobs in the federal government; in turn, potential appointees worry that the process will embarrass them.

Although potential appointees worry more about the process than actual appointees would recommend, they also worry about living in Washington, D.C., and report significant concerns about the impact of presidential service on their future careers, especially their ability to return to their previous jobs. The result is a dwindling pool of potential appointees, many of whom may be motivated more by the chance to make future contacts and increase their earning power than the chance to serve an admired president.

On top of these concerns, each Senate nominee must answer hundreds of questions about their past. They must list every job they have held over the past 15 years, the birth places of their parents, grandparents, and spouses, any significant financial conflicts they might have, all gifts they have made over $50 to their friends and associates, and identify any medical or psychological treatment they may have received. They must also list any travel abroad, including short trips to Canada and Mexico, and must give the name, address, and phone number of high school and college friends. These questionnaires take weeks to complete, and are then reviewed by the White House, the Federal Bureau of Investigation, and a variety of other government offices and the Senate.

It is no wonder that it takes so much time to build an administration. By early June, Obama had nominated barely half of the 500 appointees who will control the bureaucracy. He will be lucky if his last appointee is sworn in for service by early 2010.

Assessing the Performance of Government

Obama's third major task in taking control of the bureaucracy involved a detailed assessment of the performance of each department and agency. These assessments were conducted during the transition between the election and inauguration, and involved dozens of transition teams who were sent to every department and agency to complete their assessments.

These assessments showed trouble spots throughout the bureaucracy, especially in agencies that are essential if Obama's policy agenda is to be successful implemented. The Department of Health and Human Services was badly managed, and its Food and Drug Administration was demoralized; the Department of Homeland Security was still struggling to complete the merger of 22 agencies and 170,000 employees that had begun in 2003; the Department of the Treasury and many of the independent regulatory agencies that oversee the economy were in disarray, largely because of a lack of strong leadership in key posts at the top.

Most importantly, the federal bureaucracy was stuffed with unnecessary layers of management. Over the years, Congress and the president added new layers of management across the federal hierarchy, including dozens of new posts and seemingly useless positions such as assistant secretaries, associate deputy undersecretaries, and chiefs of staff throughout the bureaucracy.

By the time Obama became president, this "thickening" of the federal government had created the tallest and widest executive hierarchy in modern history. By 2008, the senior levels of the hierarchy contained 64 discrete executive titles and almost 2,600 titleholders, up from 51 titles and 2,400 titleholders in the final years of the Clinton administration. Although some of the growth reflects the war on terrorism, every department has added new titles to its inventory. Presidents may think the titles create greater leadership, but past research suggests just the opposite—more leaders create more opportunity for delay and lost information.

Unfortunately, the thickening has resisted all efforts to contain it. The Reagan administration lost the battle of the bulge against middle-level supervisors, and the Clinton administration appears to have created an entirely new industry in reclassifying supervisory titles into nonsupervisory titles that are still part of the chain of command. Although the Clinton administration deserves credit for cutting the number of supervisors by at least a quarter, it also merits blame for increasing the number of senior layers at the same time. If breadth does not increase, depth will, and vice versa. Both of these trends reduce the clarity of command, while increasing the distance that information must move and the potential distortions associated with ever-lengthening reporting chains.

Making Public Service "Cool" Again

Obama may have made his greatest progress in honoring his pledge to make public service attractive to young and older Americans alike. For Obama, public service runs the gamut from a day of service now and again to a year or two with AmeriCorps or Teach for America, and lifelong careers in government or charities.

Obama did more than just talk about the value of service. Working closely with Congress, he won passage of the Edward M. Kennedy Serve America Act in April 2009.

Toward encouraging more volunteerism, the act designated September 11th as an annual day of service, created Youth Engagement Zones to promote service-learning in distressed communities, and created a "Campus of Service" program designed to recognize and fund up to 25 colleges and universities for their service-learning work.

Toward supporting longer-term service, the act tripled the size of AmeriCorps, increased tuition benefits, provided the funds for a new ServeAmerica Fellowship program, and established an Encore Fellowship program for Americans age 55 and older. Each Encore Fellow is slated to receive the training to pursue a longer-term public-service career after their fellowship ends.

Obama also began hiring the thousands of new federal employees needed to implement his agenda, rebuild beleaguered agencies such as the Food and Drug Administration, and oversee his stimulus package. He also had the 2007 Loan Forgiveness Program created for college students who serve at least 10 years working for government or a charity after graduation.

Still, Obama cannot succeed in strengthening public service without the help of colleges and universities. They act as gatekeepers into the world of public service, and play a critical role in shaping student attitudes about public service of all kinds.

Too often, however, colleges and universities see volunteering as something students should do in their downtime, Americorps as little more than a ticket to graduate school, and public service careers as an inferior destination to the exhilarating, high-prestige jobs that used to exist in the private sector.

Consider these seven myths that need to be confronted by higher education as it seeks to help implement Obama's public service agenda.

1. The first myth is that public service is solely about volunteering. The Obama agenda suggests otherwise. Public service comes in many shapes and sizes, and should be presented as part of life well lived. It can take place almost anywhere, including government, charities, and businesses. It can also involve

everything from traditional social services such as serving meals at homeless shelters to inventing clean technologies. And it can involve bursts of service for a concentrated period throughout life.

Instead of embracing this multidimensional definition, many colleges and universities isolate the pieces of public service in specialized silos, such as offices of community service and career counseling. Instead of reorganizing these offices into an unwieldy whole, presidents and chancellors might create a sustainable campaign to promote all forms of engagement, while creating public-service pathways through the university curricula.

2. The second myth is that public service should be motivated by civic duty. As colleges and universities launch their annual campaigns for public service, they often fall back on the standard calls to action, built on civic duty. After all, this is how the "Greatest Generation" was called to service.

For the most part, however, such calls rarely work. Public service is better understood as a means to an end, not an end in itself. For most students, public service is not about obligation, but about the chance to make a difference on issues such as poverty, homelessness, inequality, Darfur, and global warming. Colleges and universities should structure the conversation about public service around issues that matter most to the young Americans who tuned in for the 2008 election, not around service as a movement that operates without a commitment to lasting change.

3. The third myth is that public service is always rewarding. Too often, colleges and universities focus on what students can get from service by way of a recommendation, course credit, or a future job, thereby reinforcing student expectations about immediate gratification.

The reality is that most public service involves at least some willingness to stuff envelopes and answer phones, especially early on. Public service agencies cannot provide a scintillating experience for students who show up whenever they please, nor can they survive the current economic implosion without doing menial tasks.

Colleges and universities must be honest about the kind of work students can expect. Even as the demand for service rises, charitable organizations are cutting frontline jobs wherever they can, making volunteer work more essential but perhaps less exciting. At the same time, state and local governments are imposing hiring freezes, pay furloughs, and job cuts, creating fewer opportunities for longer-term careers. For the time being, students would do well to remember that menial tasks may be the most important tasks of all. Colleges and universities should help make that case.

4. The fourth myth is that students should accept the status quo. If social programs do not work, so be it. If new ideas are constantly crushed, so be it,

too. If antiquated systems are failing, keep quiet. No matter what their task, menial or not, students should be part of something that works. Otherwise, they will walk away, never to return.

Colleges and universities should provide a different option. They should help their students imagine innovative ways of solving problems, and make those ideas more visible. The easiest way to promote this social innovation is to create relatively small investment funds to help students push their prototypes through the research and development phase, such as what New York University is doing with its annual small-grants competition open to every student on campus.

Some of these ideas may eventually earn implementation support from the federal government's new $50 million Social Innovation Fund. As Michelle Obama noted in announcing the program on May 5, 2009, "The idea is simple: find the most effective programs out there and then provide the capital needed to replicate their success in communities around the country." The federal funding merely confirms what change agents have long understood: Social innovation may be the most difficult kind of public service of all, but often starts with a spark of inspiration encouraged by a tiny grant.

5. The fifth myth is that days of service provide the essentials of a campus of service. Although days of service do produce cleaner parks, neighborhoods, and freshly painted schools, they can also reinforce the episodic, once-in-a-while volunteering that appears to be increasing among young Americans. In turn, this occasional volunteering places great stress on the organizations the young people wish to support, if only because volunteers cannot be counted on for regular schedules.

Durable commitments to public service are essential for giving students the kind of meaningful work they crave. Why invest in training when students only show up when they please? It is one thing to volunteer once a year, and quite another to show up every week to read to children or lobby for educational reform. It would be still another if Obama were to expand the day of service into a year of service that every 18-year-old must complete.

6. The sixth myth is that students should pay attention to pay, benefits, and security when they pick a public service career. It is a particularly powerful sales pitch in these difficult economic times.

There is no doubt that pay, benefits, and security must meet a minimum threshold. And a little debt relief and a reasonable work–life balance are important, too. But according to survey after survey of college seniors, the most important reasons for even considering a public service career is the chance to make a difference. Students are not saying "Show me the money," but "Show me the impact." Colleges and universities could do the public a great favor by reinforcing this message.

7. The seventh myth is that public service is for the young. Many colleges and universities focus on public service by their college-aged students. However, they increasingly enroll older Americans who return to college in preparation for "encore" careers.

These older students are often ignored in the service programs on campus. Because many go to college part-time because they are still working, they are rarely included in discussions about public service of any kind. They are not included in the advertising for volunteer work, are not part of the outreach for Americorps and other post-graduate years of service, and are left on their own in career planning. Even though the ServeAmerica act clearly encourages older Americans to pursue encore careers, most colleges and universities have yet to build programs to attract them to service.

Most colleges and universities have been slow to accept this reality. Instead, they tend to divide public service into highly specialized destinations with equally specialized curricula. As sector switching has increased, however, students need more pliable skills that will allow them to move easily from one sector to another and back again. They also need the ability to manage the networks of government, charities, and businesses that now create most public goods.

Deciding How to Decide

Obama's last challenge in taking control of the bureaucracy involved his system for making decisions. Who will be in charge of each policy question? Where will the key decisions be made? Will the bureaucracy be involved at all?

Past presidents have used one of three different approaches to making choices. One is the competitive model. It was pioneered by President Lyndon Johnson. Under the competitive model, staffers across government compete for the president's attention—the ones that have access get in, and the ones with little political power are excluded.

The second model involves an effort to build consensus among competing staff. It was first used in the modern presidency by President John F. Kennedy and was copied by President Bill Clinton. In the collegial systems, staffers work together to forge consensus on key issues. Their job is to come to agreement, even if everyone does not have equal power.

The third model involves a tight chain of command in which the president is only given the information he or she needs to make a decision. Presidents Richard M. Nixon and Ronald Reagan used the approach, forcing staffers to bring their ideas forward to a strong gatekeeper, usually the chief of staff to the president, who decides what the president should see.

Obama chose a blend of the collegial and tight chain of command approach. He wants to hear all opinions from the staff, but also limits the flow of alternative views through his office through his chief of staff. In this way, he gets to hear dissent and alternative views of each major problem. At the same time, he is protected against less important issues as Emanuel sorts through the issues as they arrive at the White House.

FIXING A BROKEN GOVERNMENT

The one item not on Obama's agenda was government reform itself. Although he did promise to "scrub" the federal budget in search of fraud, waste, and abuse, he showed little interest in a major effort to make government more effective by merging or even closing departments and agencies, changing the laws about the civil service, streamlining the presidential appointments process, or cutting the number of layers in the towering federal bureaucracy.

The problem is that Obama inherited a broken bureaucracy. In doing so, he seemed to lose sight of, or recall, Alexander Hamilton's warning about the dangers of a government ill executed. As he argued in *Federalist No. 70*: "A feeble execution is but another phrase for a bad execution; and a government ill executed, whatever it may be in theory must be in practice, a bad government."[1]

More than 200 years later, however, the federal government seems plagued by bad execution. The failures are all too familiar: counterfeit drugs and lead-painted toys, taxpayer abuse by the Internal Revenue Service, security breaches at the nation's nuclear laboratories, missing laptops at the Federal Bureau of Investigation, the *Challenger* and *Columbia* space shuttle disasters, breakdowns in policing everything from job safety to Mad Cow disease, the sluggish response to Hurricane Katrina, miscalculations about the war in Iraq, a cascade of fraudulent defense contracts, continued struggles to unite the nation's intelligence services, backlogs at dozens of agencies, shortages of air traffic controllers and food inspectors, security mistakes on airport passenger screening lines, and negligent care of veterans.

This is not to suggest that the federal government was a wasteland of failure. To the contrary, the federal government accomplishes the impossible every day. Yet, if the federal government was still far from being ill executed, it was not uniformly well executed, either.

Hamilton's warning reflected more than his own experience with an ill-executed government during the Revolutionary War.[2] He also recognized that the new government would fail unless it could execute laws. After all, the Constitution said almost nothing about the administrative state beyond giving the president a role, checked and balanced, in appointing and overseeing the officers of government. Otherwise, it was up to the president to decide how to take care that the laws would be faithfully executed. According to Hamilton, that required an energetic executive and a public service to match.[3]

So what could Obama do? Rather than tinkering at the margins with small adjustments, he could take on a major agenda of change. Although there may be benefits in taking on one problem at a time and building momentum toward government-wide action on many of the problems facing the nation, such incremental reform has stalled repeatedly in past Congresses.

Moreover, piecemeal reform merely reduces steadiness in administration, while denying the opportunity for tradeoffs that might increase the odds of action. Better to address all the problems at once than add one reform to another year after year, and better to build legislative consensus when reforms can be shaped into trades between key stakeholders such as senior executive, contractors, and frontline employees.

Rather than focusing first on specific reforms, such as cutting the number of presidential appointees, flattening the federal hierarchy, providing adequate resources for faithfully executing the laws, and making the hidden federal workforce more transparent, all of which have merit as part of a comprehensive package, the key question is how to generate enough attention to act.

The answer is an action-forcing event that produces both the urgency and the opportunity to act. The upcoming retirement of hundreds of thousands of federal employees who came into government 30 years ago provides both elements; Congress and the president will have the ability to reenergize the federal service without inflicting benefit cuts, tax increases, or both. Instead of viewing the exodus of baby boomers as a crisis, Congress and the president should view it as an opportunity.

Viewed as a problem, the coming retirements constitute a serious threat to government's ability to faithfully execute the laws. Institutional memory will decline as senior executives leave, turnover at the top and bottom of government will create gaps in service and accountability, and the thickening of government will tend to erode the chain of command.

Viewed as an opportunity, however, the coming retirements provide the opportunity to reshape federal careers, particularly if the vacancies are not automatically filled by the next federal employee in line. Evaluating each job as the occupant leaves would create the opportunity to thin the government hierarchy, shift resources downward to the front lines where government serv-ices are delivered, abandon needless reform, and renew the promise of mean-ingful work for talented Americans.

The retirement of the bureaucracy's baby boomers could also produce a much more pliable government, including a new disciplinary system that involves an end to inflated annual performance ratings, room for at least some migration of inherently governmental contractor jobs back into government, and a restoration of the federal service's reputation as an employer of choice for young Americans.

QUESTIONS TO CONSIDER

1. Why is the transition important to a president's first-year success? And why is the first year so important to a president's eventual success during the entire term?
2. How can presidents ensure that they recruit talented people for the top jobs? What are the most important qualifications for being a presidential appointee?
3. Why must the president gain control of the bureaucracy? Can the president have too much control?

NOTES

[1] Alexander Hamilton, James Madison, and John Jay, *The Federalist* (Cambridge, MA: Harvard University Press, 1961), p. 451.

[2] See Peri E. Arnold, *Making the Managerial Presidency: Comprehensive Reorganization Planning, 1905–1980* (Princeton, N.J.: Princeton University Press, 1986), for a discussion of the search for an effective administrative state.

[3] Although scholars have long assumed that the administrative state did not fully emerge until the creation of the Interstate Commerce Commission in 1887, recent research suggests that the contours of the new administrative state were visible almost immediately after George Washington became president. See Jerry L. Mashaw, "Recovering American Administrative Law: Federal Foundations, 1787–1801," *Yale Law Journal* 115 (2006), pp.1256–1344, for a summary of this view and a contrary view of the early development of the administrative state.

Chapter 5

Government and the Economy

Edward S. Greenberg

The economic collapse in the United States in 2008 and 2009 was, by all accounts, the worst since the Great Depression in the 1930s. While by no means matching the depth or duration of the Great Depression—at its worst point in early 1933 when Franklin Roosevelt assumed the presidency, the unemployment rate in the United States was 33 percent; manufacturing activity was roughly 40 percent of what it had been in the mid-1920s; thousands of banks had collapsed, taking millions of people's bank accounts with them; farm income was less than half of what it had been; and soup kitchens and bread lines were a common sight across the country—our recent economic troubles were the worst that most living Americans had ever experienced.

While the Bureau of Economic Analysis reports that the economic recession began in the fourth quarter of 2007, matters really came to a head in late summer and fall, 2008. Fannie Mae and Freddie Mac, the gigantic firms backing most mortgages in the United States, faced imminent collapse, as did the nation's largest insurance company, American International Group (AIG). The nation's best known and respected investment banks seemed to disappear overnight. Bear Stearns, Lehman Brothers, Merrill Lynch, Goldman Sachs, and Morgan Stanley, weighed down by nearly worthless mortgage-backed securities, were either liquidated, forced to merge with commercial banks, or chose to become bank holding companies in order to bring themselves under federal insurance protections. The contagion spread to seemingly safe commercial banks such as Washington Mutual (the Federal Deposit Insurance Corp., or FDIC, arranged its sale to Chase Bank), while Bank of America and Wells Fargo, among others, went right to the brink before stepping back. The collapse of the financial system led to a credit squeeze in which commercial banks and other financial institutions, burned by bad loans and burdened by their own troubled assets (most were heavily invested in near-worthless derivatives and mortgage-backed securities), cut back on lending money to individuals and businesses, or charged more for them, even for their best and most credit-worthy customers. Without access to credit, many consumers cut back on their purchases, increasing the national savings rate, to be sure, but devastating many companies, big and small, as their sales plummeted. The bankruptcies of General Motors and Chrysler were but the tip of a very large iceberg of businesses unable to weather the storm. With revenues down and access to credit severely limited, many companies put off plans to expand, and cut orders to their suppliers and laid off employees. Investors withdrew from the stock market seeking safe havens such as government bonds, treasury notes, and money market accounts.

The effects of these difficulties were reflected in all the major economic indicators. Overall economic activity contracted, with the gross domestic product (GDP) down 5.4 percent in the fourth quarter of 2008 compared to a year earlier, and down an additional 6.4 percent in the first quarter of 2009. The stock market lost over half of its value as the Dow Jones Industrial Index fell from its record high of 14,165 on October 9, 2007 to a low of 6,440 in March 2009, taking a toll on pension funds and many people's 401(k) retirement funds. Millions of people lost their homes to foreclosure as the housing market collapsed across the country, with Sunbelt states such as Florida, Arizona, and California being especially hard hit. Those avoiding foreclosure discovered their homes were worth a lot less than before, and were unwilling or unable to borrow on their equity to fund home improvements and consumer purchases. Between November 2008 and April 2009, about 645,000 Americans lost their jobs every month; between May and July 2009, monthly job losses averaged 331,000.[1] Unemployment reached just under 10 percent in September 2009, with more than one in three of those without jobs unemployed for more than 27 weeks, a record for the post-World War II United States. Average hours worked fell to 33 per week, the lowest on record,[2] as many people seeking full-time work had to settle for part-time as businesses cut back. While the economic collapse may well have reached bottom by the fall of 2009, no one was expecting a rapid rebound or a dramatic improvement on the employment front for many months to come.

The federal government intervened in new and big ways in response to the Great Depression, and the same thing happened, and continues, in the midst of the current economic crisis. Though Franklin Roosevelt's New Deal is best remembered as the main government response to the Great Depression, it is worth remembering that conservative Republican Herbert Hoover, president for the first three years or so of that economic and financial crisis, successfully pushed for legislation to increase funding to the states for their poor-relief efforts; he created the Reconstruction Finance Corporation to subsidize loans to imperiled banks and large companies facing collapse, and brought the leaders of big business together to form voluntary cooperative alliances to write "codes of fair trade" to dampen competition, raise prices, and increase profits.[3] But it was Roosevelt's New Deal that transformed the role of government in the American government and economy, and changed the average citizen's conception of what the role of the federal government should be. After Roosevelt, no American president could simply stand by and let the free market "sort out the mess." Essentially, the New Deal created a set of institutions and programs to enhance the security of the financial system, put people to work, provide small pensions for the elderly and disabled (the Social Security Act), and improve the infrastructure of the American economy.[4] Roosevelt began by declaring a bank holiday, allowing only sound banks to reopen, and then pushed through Congress the Glass-Steagall Banking Act of 1933, which separated investment and commercial banking (preventing banks from wildly speculating with depositors' money), and guaranteed depositors' savings and checking accounts up to $5,000 (a not-insignificant sum in 1933), thus ending bank runs by panicky depositors. The Securities and Exchange Commission was created to regulate away some of the most dangerous practices on Wall Street and to make corporate operations more transparent to potential investors. The creation of the Home Owners Loan Association and the Federal National Mortgage Association made home ownership more available and affordable for a broad range of Americans. Railroads, airline companies, and public utilities came under federal regulation, as did radio broadcasting, bringing stability, predictability, and long-term profitability to firms in these industries. (Unfortunately, innovation may have suffered to a degree, a factor that contributed to the deregulation movement of the 1980s and 1990s.) Unemployed people were put to work in a range of alphabet programs: the Civilian Conservation Corps (CCC), the Works Project Administration (WPA), and the Public Works Administration (PWA), among others. The Tennessee Valley Authority was created, bringing electricity to large areas of the South for the first time.

New Deal programs also, in the words of historian David Kennedy, "succored the indigent and patronized the arts. It built roads, bridges, and hospitals. It added twelve million acres of national parklands, including Olympic National Park in Washington state, Isle Royal in Lake Superior, the Everglades in Florida, and King's Canyon in California. It planted trees and fought erosion. It erected mammoth dams—Grand Coulee and Bonneville on the Columbia, Shasta on the Sacramento, Fort Peck on the Missouri—that were river tamers and nature busters, to be sure, but jobmakers and region-builders too."[5]

The New Deal represented a dramatic change in the role of the national government in American life and in the management of the American economy. It may well be that responses to the current emergency will also transform many aspects of federal policy and the role of the federal government in the United States. There were already hints of this in the response of the federal government during the last nine months or so of George W. Bush's presidency. Though a Republican and a self-described conservative, his administration responded in a surprisingly vigorous manner, rather than leaving the emergency to the tonic of the free market. Bush and the Democratic Congress passed an economic stimulus package in February 2008, as indications of a growing recession were becoming more apparent. The stimulus was a combination of temporary tax rebates and added government spending amounting to $152 billion, designed to increase spending by individuals and firms. The Federal Reserve, headed by Bush appointee Ben Bernanke, aggressively cut short-term interest rates throughout the spring, summer, and fall to stimulate economic activity, and stepped up its lending to banks in an attempt to head off troubles in the financial system. But the financial system, burdened with mortgage-backed securities in the middle of a collapse in the real estate market, had come close to the precipice by the early fall. To head off disaster, the Federal Reserve (the Fed) in a somewhat surprising and unconventional move, arranged and partially paid for J.P. Morgan's purchase of the failing investment bank Bear Stearns, as well as for Bank of America's absorption of troubled Merrill Lynch. The Treasury Department, led by Secretary Hank Paulson, and the Federal Reserve, together bailed out Fannie Mae and Freddie Mac to the tune of $25 billion (it had reached $85 billion by the end of summer 2009), then pumped more than $100 billion into AIG. The FDIC arranged and helped subsidize JP Morgan's purchase of Washington Mutual, one of the nation's most important commercial banks. The FDIC also tried to settle people's jitters by increasing the maximum level of insurance protection it would provide for deposits from $100,000 to $250,000.

These piecemeal efforts, though substantial in terms of the small government, deregulation, low-tax philosophy dominant in the country since the Reagan Revolution of the early 1980s, were clearly not enough. In mid-September, Bernanke and Paulson, worried that the American economy was on the brink of disaster because of a deep and rapidly spreading credit freeze, convinced President Bush and Congress to pass a massive $700 billion rescue package directed primarily at the nation's largest financial institutions. The idea was to buy up the nearly worthless assets of the nation's major financial institutions (mostly, but not entirely, mortgage-backed securities) and infuse massive amounts of new money into them, freeing them up to begin lending again to individuals and companies, and restoring confidence in them among investors in the United States and abroad. Despite these actions, the economy was in terrible straits by the end of 2008, with the stock market in free fall (the Dow lost 18 percent of its value during the first week of October), economic growth going backwards, banks refusing or unable to lend money—even to each other, companies failing (including Linens-n-Things, The Sharper Image, Levitz Furniture, and Mervyns), unemployment rising, and consumer confidence at one of its lowest points ever. In a remarkable step, unable to get the financial system on its feet, and following the lead of Great Britain and the European Union, Bernanke and Paulson decided to use a portion of the just-passed $700 billion bailout package to inject money into the financial system by buying up ownership shares in banks and other financial institutions, in effect, partially nationalizing them. In doing this, these two Bush appointees had moved a considerable distance from the free market philosophy that had dominated Washington policies for over 20 years.[6]

Though the national tides were running in their direction since at least 2006, the economic crisis that came to a head in the middle of the 2008 election campaign contributed mightily to the Democrats' landslide victory, with Barack Obama winning the presidency over John McCain by a healthy margin and Democrats increasing their control over Congress (as well as state legislatures). And most congressional Democrats (though not all) and President Obama wanted, and promised, some very big changes in the role of government. Some of the changes were designed to deal with the immediate economic crisis. For example, Congress passed a $787 billion stimulus bill (for which not a single Republican in the House voted), which the president signed on February 17, 2009, less than 30 days from the date of his inauguration. The stimulus package was a combination of tax cuts and new expenditures in programs that, among other things, extended unemployment benefits, funded new research and development in alternative energy sources, put monies into school construction, and massively increased infrastructure projects (i.e., roads, bridges, canals, and the like). Other changes were tied to fixing some of the problems that caused the financial meltdown, particularly mortgage securitization and subprime mortgage loans, and were regulatory in nature.

Though financial sector regulatory reform has not yet happened in Congress, the Treasury Department announced deep cuts in executive pay at companies that had not yet repaid government bailout monies, and the Fed announced new policies to monitor and publicize executive pay at thousands of banks. And, perhaps most consequentially, the president proposed fundamental changes in the nation's health care system and pressed for a "cap and trade" system to address global warming and energy independence. At this writing, a health care reform bill to President Obama's liking is close to passage in Congress, though the climate change bill's prospects are less certain.

Not surprisingly, the present economic crisis has fostered a substantial increase in the federal government's role in the American economy. This has developed not only during the liberal Democratic administration of Barack Obama, but also during the conservative Republican George W. Bush administration. The trend is likely to continue in the near future—despite news that the American economy began to grow again in late 2009—because it will take some time for unemployment and foreclosures to turn around. When Americans are hurting, it seems, they want their government to take steps to improve things.

QUESTIONS TO CONSIDER

1. Who is most to blame for the financial crisis of 2009 and the deep recession of 2009 and 2010?
2. Do you believe the federal government should play a bigger role in managing the economy, or should we rely more on the free market for sustained economic growth and rising living standards?
3. Are you concerned about the growing federal deficits as government (under both George W. Bush and Barack Obama) has increased spending to cover financial and corporate bailouts and loan guarantees, extended unemployment payments and various economic stimulus programs? Why or why not? If so, what solutions would you offer? Increase taxes to cover deficits? Cut back on emergency economic programs? Cut major entitlements such as Social Security and Medicare?

NOTES

[1]National Bureau of Economic Analysis, "National Income and Product Accounts" (Washington, DC: U.S. Department of Commerce, press release, July 31, 2009).

[2]The Bureau of Labor Statistics only began using this statistic in 1964.

[3]Edward S. Greenberg, *Serving the Few* (New York: John Wiley and Sons, 1974), pp. 111, 113.

[4]For all of this, see David M. Kennedy, *Freedom From Fear: The American People in Depression and War, 1929–1945,* (New York: Oxford University Press, 1999), chap. 12.

[5]Ibid., p. 379.

[6]Bill Clinton, the only Democratic president during this period, was proudest of having balanced the federal budget. He even famously said in his 1996 State of the Union address that "the era of big government is over."

Chapter 6

A Full Plate: The Obama Policy Agenda

Thomas R. Dye

CRISIS AS INSPIRATION

"**N**ever allow a crisis to go to waste. Crises are opportunities to do big things."[1] This comment by White House Chief of Staff Rahm Emanuel characterizes the approach of President Barack Obama and his administration in developing a policy agenda for the first year in office. The Obama policy agenda is extensive, ranging from a bailout of the nation's financial institutions, government investment in the auto industry, changes in the tax structure, and a huge increase in federal spending and deficit levels; to a transformation of the nation's health care system, energy and environmental initiatives, comprehensive immigration reform, and shifts in national defense policy. Not all of these policy changes are to be accomplished in a year, yet all have been outlined in early presidential messages as well as the 2010 Budget of the United States Government.

THE FINANCIAL CRISIS

For years Americans lived on easy credit. Families ran up credit card debt and borrowed heavily for cars, tuition, and especially homebuying. Mortgage lenders approved loans for borrowers without fully examining their ability to pay and often with little or no down payment. Federally chartered corporations, Fanny Mae and Freddy Mac, encouraged mortgage loans to low-income and minority homebuyers. Some mortgages were "predatory" with initial low payments followed by steep upward adjustable rates. Financial institutions seeking quick profits developed a nationwide market in "subprime mortgages." Risk was frequently ignored. To make matters worse, banks and financial institutions bundled mortgages together and sold these mortgage-backed securities as "derivatives." Banks, insurers, and lenders all assumed that housing prices would inevitably rise.

But eventually the bubble burst: Housing prices fell dramatically. Homeowners found themselves holding "upside down" mortgages—mortgages that exceeded the value of their homes. Many were unable or unwilling to meet their mortgage payments. Foreclosures and delinquencies spiraled upward. Investors who held mortgage-backed securities began to incur heavy losses. Investment banks and mortgage insurers found themselves in serious financial trouble. The stock market plummeted.

Wall Street Bailout. In 2008 Wall Street faced its biggest crisis since the Great Depression. Hundreds of billions of dollars in mortgage-related investments went bad and many of the nation's leading investment banks and insurance companies sought the assistance of the Treasury Department and the Federal Reserve System. The Fed acted to stave off bankruptcy of Bear Stearns and the Treasury Department took over Fannie Mae and Freddie Mac. The Fed bailed out American International Group (AIG), the nation's largest insurance company. But the hemorrhaging continued, and it was soon clear that the nation was tumbling into a deep recession.

In September 2008, the treasury secretary and the Federal Reserve chairman went before Congress to plead for a massive $700 billion bailout of banks, insurance companies, and investment firms that held mortgage-backed "illiquid assets." They argued that their proposal was absolutely essential to safeguard the financial security of the nation. The nation's top leadership, including presidential candidates Senator Barack Obama and Senator John McCain, supported the bill. But polls showed that most Americans opposed a "Wall Street Bailout." The House of Representatives initially voted no. But predictions of economic catastrophe inspired the Senate to pass the bill by a comfortable margin, and in a sharp reversal of its earlier action, the House approved the Emergency Economic Stabilization Act of 2008.

Treasury's TARP. The Treasury Department was given unprecedented power to bail out the nation's financial institutions. The program was named the Troubled Asset Relief Program (TARP). The nation's largest bank, Citigroup, was the first in line and other major banks and investment firms followed (see Table 1). Government loans were secured by preferred stock shares.

Critics of the program noted that by accepting ownership shares in the nation's leading banks and investment houses, the government was tilting toward "socialism." Government ownership shares of financial institutions, that is, "nationalization" of the banks, would have been considered unthinkable before this crisis.

Mortgage Modification. Under President Obama's new treasury secretary, Timothy Geithner, banks receiving TARP assistance were obliged to adopt mortgage loan modification procedures to prevent or forestall foreclosures. To be eligible borrowers had to show "hardship." The intention was to aid as many as five million mortgage borrowers who were in default to refinance their loans at lower interest rates. Critics of the program expressed a fear of rising resentment among the millions of Americans who sacrificed to keep current on their mortgage payments.

Public-Private Investment Program. The key to loosening credit and jumpstarting the economy appeared to be relieving the nation's banks of their "toxic" assets—securities backed by mortgages that were in foreclosure or default. A Public-Private Investment Program uses TARP money to leverage private purchases of these assets; the Federal Deposit Insurance Corp. and the Federal Reserve System facilitate private purchases by providing low-interest loans to buyers of these assets. By relieving banks of these "nonperforming" loans, they should then be prepared to make new loans and thereby stimulate the economy. The potential cost to the government may run up to $1 trillion.

Table 1. Top Federal Bailout Recipients

American International Group (AIG)
Citigroup
JP Morgan Chase
Wells Fargo
Bank of America
Goldman Sachs
Merrill Lynch
Morgan Stanley
PNC Financial Services
US Bancorp

GM Bankruptcy. General Motors is an American institution, the biggest of the "Big Three" domestic automobile manufacturers—GM, Chrysler, and Ford. With federal supervision, GM and Chrysler sought bankruptcy protection in 2009; Ford managed to stay afloat by itself. Even before declaring bankruptcy, General Motors had received billions of federal dollars in loans and loan guarantees. Federal involvement forced out GM's chief executive officer. In bankruptcy, the federal government took majority ownership of GM. President Obama declared that the federal government had no interest in the day-to-day operations of General Motors. Yet the White House issued guidelines for limiting the salaries of top executives of GM and of other institutions receiving TARP funds.

Greater Financial Regulation. The Obama administration has proposed a series of new regulatory measures designed to avoid future financial crisis.

These include a new oversight agency to protect consumers from predatory and deceptive credit card and mortgage loan practices; new authority for the Federal Reserve to oversee banks and investment firms and other institutions considered "too big to fail"; and a new council of federal regulators, chaired by the treasury secretary, to monitor risk across the broader financial market.

THE ECONOMIC STIMULUS PACKAGE

A massive economic stimulus plan, officially the American Recovery and Reinvestment Act of 2009, was the centerpiece of President Obama's early policy agenda. Its combination of spending increases and tax cuts totaled $757 billion—the largest single fiscal policy measure in American history. Written in record time by a Democratic-controlled Congress, House Republicans were unanimous in opposition, and only three Republican senators supported the bill.

Spending Priorities. The stimulus package consisted of roughly two-thirds spending and one-third tax rebates. Democrats in Congress used the package to increase spending in a wide variety of domestic programs—education, Medicaid, unemployment compensation, food stamps, health technology, child tax credits, disability payments, higher education grants, renewable energy subsidies, and rail and transit—as well as traditional spending for highways and bridge building (see Table 2). Republicans complained that much of the spending had little to do with stimulating the economy, but instead only increased government involvement in domestic policy areas favored by liberals and Democrats. Republicans traditionally preferred to rely upon tax cuts to stimulate the economy.

Tax "Cuts." The stimulus package also included a version of Obama's campaign promise of a middle-class tax cut. The tax cuts in the package, labeled "Making Work Pay," were actually payments of $400 to individuals with incomes under $75,000, and payments of $800 to couples with incomes under $150,000. These payments were made to anyone who paid Social Security taxes. It was not necessary to have paid any income taxes in order to receive these tax cuts. Critics labeled these payments "welfare checks."

The stimulus package was initially presented to Congress as an emergency measure requiring quick passage in order to deal with a deepening recession. But President Obama had recommended many of its provisions to Congress as permanent measures in his very first budget message. Making Work Pay tax payments were repackaged as "the first stage" of Obama's middle-class tax cut promise, made during his presidential campaign. These payments are designed to partly offset the Social Security payroll tax (FICA).

REDISTRIBUTING INCOME VIA THE TAX CODE

Barack Obama campaigned on a promise to lower taxes on the middle class, which he defined as 95 percent of taxpayers. He also pledged to raise taxes on upper-income Americans, which he defined as families earning $250,000 a year or more. This combination of changes in taxation would make the Tax Code more progressive.

Raising Taxes on the Rich. The Bush tax cuts had been scheduled to expire at the end of 2010. Republicans argued that allowing these tax cuts to become permanent would result in a tax increase. But Democrats and President Obama argued that the expiration of these cuts would simply return taxes to their previous levels—raising the top marginal tax rate from 35 to 39.6 percent. President Obama also recommended a phaseout of deductions, including charitable contributions and mortgage payments, for families making over $250,000. Congress appeared less enthusiastic about the phaseout of these deductions.

Income Redistribution. The combination of these changes in the Tax Code—tax payments to lower- and middle-income families and an increase in the top marginal tax rate—has the effect of redistributing after-tax income among Americans. Critics charge that redistribution income is socialism, which penalizes work, initiative, and talent. Americans generally believe in tax progressivity—higher income people can afford to be taxed at larger percentages of their added incomes than lower income people. But deliberate attempts by government to use the Tax Code to equalize income represents a new direction in tax policy.

Table 2. The Stimulus Package

Major categories of items in the American Recovery and Reinvestment Act of 2009.

- Tax payments: $400 to individuals with incomes under $75,000, and $800 to couples with incomes under $150,000.
- State Medicaid assistance
- Education and job training aid to school districts
- Unemployment compensation: increase and extension to 33 weeks
- Highways and bridges: money to states for "shovel ready" projects
- Health care for unemployed: health insurance for unemployed for 9 months
- Food Stamp Program increases
- Index the Alternative Minimum Tax for inflation

- Health technology grants and subsidies
- Renewable energy grants and subsidies
- Child care tax credits
- Pell Grant increases
- Health science research
- Extend Hope Scholarships from 2 years to 4 years
- Increase Title I education monies
- Increase aid for special education
- Rail transportation and public transit

Total: $787 Billion

GROWING GOVERNMENT

The Obama policy agenda involves massive new government spending and huge federal deficits. For years, federal government spending rose more or less incrementally, remaining close to 22 percent of the Gross Domestic Product (GDP). But in 2009 federal spending rose by almost $1 trillion from the previous year, the largest single year-to-year increase in history. Federal spending in that year rose to almost 28 percent of the GDP. That same year, federal revenues declined; the extra spending was financed through a $1.7 trillion deficit, the largest annual deficit in history. The bulk of these increases in spending and deficit levels can be attributed to the fiscal crisis and the stimulus package designed to offset the sagging economy. But high levels of federal spending and deficits are projected to continue even after 2010. Critics contend that spending and deficit levels of this magnitude threaten the long-term well-being of the economy and place heavy burdens on future generations.

HEALTH CARE TRANSFORMATION

President Obama has proposed a major overhaul of the nation's health care system, a project attempted unsuccessfully by past presidents including Franklin Delano Roosevelt, Harry Truman, and Bill Clinton. In the president's words, "Moving to provide all Americans with health insurance is not only a moral imperative, but it is also essential to a more effective and efficient health care system."[2] Among the many health care proposals on the Obama agenda: expanding the State Children's Health Insurance Program (SCHIP), computerizing the nation's health records, and extending Consolidated Omnibus Budget Reconciliation Act (COBRA) health insurance to unemployed workers. Obama promises that in this health care transformation the Medicare, Medicaid, and Veterans Administration health care programs will remain unchanged. The transformed system will continue to rely primarily on private health insurance companies. However, private insurers will no longer be permitted to deny insurance for pre-existing conditions, or to drop coverage when patients get sick, and they will be required to provide for routine checkups and preventative care. These particular reforms face no serious opposition.

National Health Insurance Exchange. The president also proposes a National Health Insurance Exchange, bringing individuals and small businesses together as a group to better negotiate with insurance companies in a competitive marketplace. Individuals and small businesses will be able to bargain for affordable insurance in the fashion of large businesses and government employees.

"The Public Option." The central reform in the Obama health care agenda is the creation of a government-run "public option" as part of the national health insurance exchange. This public not-for-profit health insurance program would function side-by-side with private health insurance. Premiums are likely to be based on a sliding scale according to income. According the president, this public plan would not put private insurers out of business, but would "keep them honest" by offering reasonable coverage at affordable prices.

Critics view the public option as a "government takeover" of the nation's health care system. As a not-for-profit government-run agency, the public plan would have a competitive advantage over private insurers. Gradually, private insurance companies would lose out to this public program, over time creating a single national health insurance system or "socialized medicine." (Indeed, some critics believe this is the true intent of President Obama.)

Individual Mandate? In order to implement comprehensive reform, President Obama has also considered an individual mandate—a requirement that all Americans acquire basic health insurance. He compares this mandate to the requirement in most states for all drivers to carry auto insurance.

Cost. President Obama asserts that the costs of health care reform can be recovered in savings by changing the existing health care system—"a system that is currently full of waste and abuse." The president claims that eliminating waste and inefficiency in Medicare and Medicaid will pay for most of his plan. But critics doubt that such savings exist. Indeed, the proposal to cut waste and abuse in Medicare has inspired critics to claim that health care reform is going to come at the expense of the elderly. The Congressional Budget Office estimates the cost of Obama's health care reform proposals at nearly $1 trillion.

Presidential Lobbying. President Obama has left many of the critical details of health care reform to Congress to develop and enact. He has been largely absent from direct congressional lobbying on behalf of any specific bills or proposals (to the frustration of some of his liberal supporters). Rather, the president has chosen to rally the grassroots in speeches and town meetings across the country to inspire general support for broad principles of health care reform.

Table 3. The Growth of Government Spending

Obama's 2010 budget calls for more than $3.5 trillion in federal spending, an amount over 24% of the GDP.

	Federal Government Spending $ Billions	Percentage of GDP
1975	332	22.0
1985	946	23.8
1995	1,539	22.5
2000	1,788	18.1
2005	2,472	19.8
2008	2,983	21.0
2009	3,998	28.1
2010	3,591	24.4

Sources: Statistical Abstract of the United States, 2008; Budget of the United States Government, 2010.

CAP AND TRADE

In his first budget message to Congress, President Obama recommended an innovative approach to energy policy. In addition to pledging new federal subsidies for research and development in clean energy technologies, he proposed a new carbon emissions ceiling and trading program known as "cap and trade."[3]

A Ceiling on Carbon Emissions. The cap and trade program envisions the federal government setting overall national ceilings on carbon emissions. (The Environmental Protection Agency paved the way in 2009 by officially declaring carbon dioxide a pollutant, subject to government regulation.) The government would then hold a national auction in which polluting industries and firms could purchase tradable emissions allowances. The total amount of emission allowances auctioned off would not exceed the national ceiling or "cap." In effect, industries would be purchasing allowances to pollute. Polluting industries could keep polluting, but at a price that would encourage them to invest in reducing carbon emissions.

Relying in Part on the Market Mechanism. Firms that are successful in reducing emissions can then sell their allowances to other firms. Because the cap and trade approach relies in part on the market mechanism, it is sometimes labeled "free-market environmentalism." Setting the overall cap is a regulatory measure, but individual firms are free to choose how or if they will reduce their emissions. The system encourages innovation by individual firms. If they are successful in reducing their emissions, they can sell their allowances to other firms.

Costs to Consumers. The costs of the cap and trade program would be borne by all energy users. The costs to energy consumers would be largely invisible, passed on by industries in the form of price increases. Everything from gasoline prices to electric bills would incorporate industry costs for emission allowances at auction or in trades.

IMMIGRATION REFORM

The Obama agenda includes comprehensive immigration reform. But over the years conflict in Washington over immigration policy has been intense. To date, conflicting interests have prevented any effective action to halt illegal immigration, or to determine the status of millions of illegal immigrants already living in the United States. Among the diverse interests with a stake in immigration policy: employers seeking to keep immigration as open as possible to lower their labor costs; millions of illegal immigrants seeking a legal path to citizenship; and citizens seeking border security and opposed to "amnesty" for illegal aliens.

"Comprehensive" Reform. Comprehensive immigration reform implies compromises among various interests. In 2007, Congress considered a comprehensive bill cosponsored by Senators Edward M. Kennedy and John McCain, which included the following major provisions: strengthening border enforcement, including funding of 700 miles of fencing; granting legal status to millions of undocumented immigrants currently living in the country; providing a path to citizenship that includes criminal background checks, paying of fees, and acquiring English proficiency; establishing a temporary (two-year) guest worker program; shifting the criteria for illegal immigration from family-based preferences to a greater emphasis on skills and education. Opponents of one or another of these various provisions, both Democrats and

Republicans, united to defeat the bill in the Senate. Nonetheless, Obama's immigration reform proposals are likely to follow the broad outlines of the Kennedy-McCain bill.

SHIFTING FROM IRAQ TO AFGHANISTAN

In the presidential campaign of 2008 Barack Obama pledged to end the war in Iraq "responsibly." Upon taking office in January 2009, he ordered the U.S. military to plan for a phased withdrawal of American combat forces from Iraq. The expectation was that the United States would redeploy combat brigades at a pace of one to two per month over a 16-month period, ending in the summer of 2010. A "residual force" was to remain in Iraq—to conduct targeted counterterrorism missions against Al Qaeda, to protect American diplomatic and civilian personnel, and to continue to train and support Iraqi security forces.

Reliance on Diplomacy. The thrust of U.S. policy in the region was to shift from military to diplomatic efforts. The phased withdrawal itself was expected to encourage Iraqis to provide for their own security and to work toward real political reconciliation among its factions. The political tasks expected of the Iraqis included compromises on oil revenue sharing, equitable provision of services, continued reform of security forces, and the elimination of corruption in government. Obama also pledged to try to achieve comprehensive stability in the region by negotiating with Iran and Syria.

Shifting Focus to Afghanistan. Even while campaigning for the presidency, Obama drew a sharp distinction between the war in Iraq and the war in Afghanistan. Iraq, he claimed, had diverted America's attention away from the greater dangers posed by Al Qaeda and the Taliban forces in Afghanistan. It was Al Qaeda that was responsible for the September 11, 2001 attacks on New York's World Trade Center and the Pentagon, and it was the Taliban regime in Afghanistan that provided Al Qaeda with safe haven.

Al Qaeda and Taliban Resurgence. Shortly after entering the White House, President Obama ordered a strategic review of the situation in Afghanistan and Pakistan. The review concluded that the situation was "increasingly perilous," with Al Qaeda and its Taliban allies controlling large sections of both Afghanistan and Pakistan. The president ordered additional combat brigades to be sent to Afghanistan and additional funds to be provided to Pakistan for the training of its army and police forces.

Counterinsurgency Operations. The announced goal of U.S. policy is now to "disrupt, dismantle and defeat" Al Qaeda in both Afghanistan and Pakistan. Economic and military aid to Pakistan is to be contingent upon that country's commitment to its own security and its willingness to "confront violent extremists." American forces in Afghanistan are committed to "asymmetrical" warfare tactics—confronting lightly armed, irregular enemy forces engaging in tactics such as ambushes, hidden explosives, suicide bombings, and hostage takings. Secretary of Defense Robert Gates (held over from the Bush administration) and the nation's military leadership are committed to reconfiguring U.S. forces for asymmetric warfare—expanding the size of the Army and Marine Corps in recognition of the need for more "boots on the ground"; transforming a division-based army into one organized into brigade combat teams; introducing new equipment including Mine Resistant Ambush Protection vehicles and unmanned aerial vehicles capable of both reconnaissance and attack missions; and revising counterinsurgency doctrine to shift away from "enemy-centric" conflict toward a "population-centric" approach, emphasizing political goals and the importance of social and cultural factors in military operations.

Limited Objectives. U.S. policy now recognizes that Afghanistan's 25 million people are divided along ethnic lines. The central government in Kabul exercises little control over a country the size of Texas. The objective of U.S. policy is not necessarily to bring Western-style democracy to a united Afghanistan, but rather, to ensure that the country does not become a safe haven for Al Qaeda and their terrorist allies.

GOVERNMENT AS THE SOLUTION

In an earlier era, President Ronald Reagan set the tone of American politics: "Government is not the solution. Government is the problem." But economic crises drives Americans to seek the security of government. Under the Obama rhetoric of "change," governnment becomes the solution. Crises provide opportunities to expand government across a broad range of policy areas. If there is an underlying theme to the Obama policy agenda, it is that an activist government is indeed the solution.

QUESTIONS TO CONSIDER

1. Should the federal government bail out banks and financial institutions that have made bad decisions about loans and mortgages? Should the federal government take ownership shares in General Motors or other firms deemed "too big to fail"?
2. Is the federal government growing too big? Do massive new spending programs and huge federal deficits endanger the nation's economy in the future?

3. Do we need a "public option"—a government-run health insurance program for all citizens—in order to truly reform health care in America?

NOTES

[1]*Time*, June 15, 2009, p. 26.

[2]Office of Management and Budget, *Budget of the United States Government 2010*, p. 28 at http://www.whitehouse.gov/omb/ (date accessed November 2, 2009).

[3]Bracken Hendricks and Van Jones, "Building a Vibrant Low-Carbon Economy," in *Change for America: A Progressive Blueprint for the 44th President*, Mark Green and Michelle Jolin, eds. (New York: Basic Books, 2009), pp. 213–226.

Chapter 7

Creating Opportunities for Policy Change?

George C. Edwards III

Every president requires a strategy for governing, for bringing about changes in public policy. Recent presidents have typically sought public support for themselves and their policies that they could leverage to obtain backing for their proposals in Congress. This approach to governing rests on the premise that presidents can create opportunities to move in new directions and lead others where they otherwise would not go. The president is out in front, establishing goals and encouraging others inside and outside of government to follow. He creates a constituency to follow his lead, reshaping the contours of the political landscape to pave the way for change.

Barack Obama entered the presidency with an impressive record of political success, at the center of which were his rhetorical skills. In college, he concluded that words had the power to transform: "With the right words everything could change—South Africa, the lives of ghetto kids just a few miles away, my own tenuous place in the world."[1] Moreover, his administration was poised to exploit new means of communicating with the American public.

As president, Teddy Roosevelt gave prominence to the bully pulpit by exploiting the hunger of modern newspapers for national news. Franklin D. Roosevelt (FDR) broadened the reach and immediacy of presidential communications with his use of radio. More recently, John F. Kennedy and Ronald Reagan mastered the use of television to speak directly to the American people. Now Barack Obama has positioned himself as the first Internet president.

Following his election, it was commonplace for commentators to argue that President Obama could exploit the capacity for social networking to reach people directly in a way that television and radio cannot, and harness this potential to overcome obstacles to legislative success. References to the president's "charisma" and oratorical gifts abound. Moreover, one might conclude that in a time of severe economic crisis, when Americans are seeking reassurance from the White House, he has both the public's ear and its good wishes.

On November 18, about 10 million of Barack Obama's supporters found an e-mail message from his campaign manager, David Plouffe. Labeled "Where we go from here," Plouffe asked backers to "help shape the future of this movement" by answering an online survey, which in turn asked them to rank four priorities in order of importance. First on the list was: "Helping Barack's administration pass legislation through grassroots efforts."[2]

COMMUNICATE MORE EFFECTIVELY

This e-mail message revealed much about Barack Obama's initial approach to governing. The new administration was oriented to exploiting advances in technology to communicate with the public more effectively than ever before. Bush State Department spokesman Sean McCormack started filing posts from far-flung regions in 2008 during trips with his boss, Secretary of State Condoleezza Rice. On October 31, 2008, McCormack unveiled "Briefing 2.0" in the press briefing room of the State Department, in which he took questions from the public rather than the press and then put the session on YouTube.[3]

Yet the new occupants of the White House were oriented to exploiting the emerging technology more systematically. Obama announced his intent to seek the presidency via Web video, revealed his vice presidential selection via text message, recruited about 13 million online supporters during the campaign, and used the electronic medium to sidestep mainstream media and speak directly with voters throughout the primaries and general-election campaign. This practice forged a firsthand connection, and may have encouraged some supporters to feel a greater stake in the campaign's success. Some Obama videos have become YouTube phenomena: Millions of people have viewed his speech on the Reverend Jeremiah A. Wright Jr. and race in America, and his victory speech in Grant Park on November 4, 2008.

"It's really about reaching an extra person or a larger audience of people who wouldn't normally pay attention to policy," said Jen Psaki, a spokeswoman for Obama's transition team. "We have to think creatively about how we would do that in the White House, because promoting a speech in front of 100,000 people is certainly different than promoting energy legislation."[4]

Even before taking office, the president-elect began making Saturday radio addresses—but with a twist. In addition to beaming his addresses to radio stations nationwide, he recorded them for digital video and audio downloads from YouTube, iTunes, and the like. As a result, people could access it whenever and wherever they wanted. "Turning the weekly radio address from audio to video and making it on-demand has turned the radio address from a blip on the radar to something that can be a major newsmaking event any Saturday we choose," declared Dan Pfeiffer, the incoming White House deputy communications director. It is also easy to produce: A videographer can record Obama delivering the address in fewer than 15 minutes.[5] After his inauguration, the White House put the president's Saturday videos on both the White House Web site and a White House channel on YouTube.

The Obama White House produces and distributes much more video than any past administration. To do so, it maintains an entire staff devoted to producing online videos for whitehouse, Obama's YouTube channel, and other video depots. A search for "Barack Obama" is stacked with videos approved and uploaded by the campaign or the administration (which viewers may not realize). When filming a presidential speech, the production team tailors the video to the site, with titles, omissions, crowd cutaways, highlight footage, and a dozen other manipulations of sound and image that affected the impression they make, including applause that is difficult to edit out.[6]

In addition, the Internet, which emerged in 2008 as a leading source for campaign news, has now surpassed all other media except television as a main source for national and international news. More people now say they rely mostly on the Internet for news than cite newspapers.[7] Young people are even more likely than others to report that they rely on the Internet as a main source of national and international news. Overall, 31 percent of Americans now use the Internet as a daily news source, marking a nearly 50 percent increase since 2006.[8]

Obama made the case for his economic agenda in a variety of forums, including the *Tonight Show*, *60 Minutes*, and a prime-time news conference. On March 26, 2009, he added a new arrow to his quiver. The president held an "Open for Questions" town hall meeting in the East Room of the White House. Presidents Bill Clinton and George W. Bush answered questions over the Internet, but Obama was the first to do so in a live video format, streamed directly onto the White House Web site.

For more than an hour, the president answered questions culled from 104,000 sent over the Internet. Online voters cast more than 3.5 million votes for their favorite questions, some of which were then posed to the president by an economic adviser who served as a moderator. The president took other queries from a live audience of about 100 nurses, teachers, businesspeople, and others assembled at the White House.

The questions covered topics such as health care, education, the economy, the auto industry, and housing. In most cases, Obama used his answers to advocate his policies. The White House was not in complete control, however. One of the questions that drew the most votes online was whether legalizing marijuana might stimulate the economy by allowing the government to regulate and tax the drug. (The White House listed them on its Web site under the topics "green jobs and energy" and "budget." White House officials later indicated that interest groups drove up those reported vote numbers).[9]

When health care reform stalled in the summer, the president tried to reenergize Web-savvy allies who backed Obama in the election. He appeared in a six-minute video on the WhiteHouse.gov Web site, recounting some of the personal stories of average Americans. The administration also unveiled a new Web site dedicated to rebutting criticism of health care legislation.

Reaching people is useful for political leaders, but mobilizing them is better. Plouffe's emphasis on helping the Obama administration pass legislation through grassroots efforts indicates a desire to use public support to move Congress to support the president's program. According to Andrew Rasiej, cofounder of the Personal Democracy Forum, a nonpartisan Web site focused on the intersection of politics and technology, Obama "created his own special interest group because the same people that made phone calls on behalf of him [in the campaign] are now going to be calling or e-mailing their congressman."[10] A Pew study during the transition found that among those who voted for Obama, 62 percent expected to ask others to support at least some of the new administration's policies.[11]

Plouffe did not take a formal role in the White House. He did, however, begin overseeing the president's sprawling grassroots political operation, which boasts 13 million e-mail addresses, 4 million cell phone contacts, and 2 million active volunteers[12] (and has remained as an advisor). More than 500,000 completed surveys following the election to express their vision for the administration, and more than 4,200 hosted house parties in their communities. On January 17, 2009, Obama sent a YouTube video to supporters to announce plans to establish Organizing for America (OFA), which will enlist community organizers around the country to support local candidates, lobby for the president's agenda, and remain connected with his supporters from the campaign. There was speculation that the organization could have an annual budget of $75 million in privately raised funds and deploy hundreds of paid staff members. It was to operate from the Democratic National Committee headquarters but with an independent structure, budget, and priorities.[13]

During the transition, the Obama team drew on high-tech organizational tools to lay the groundwork for an attempt to restructure the U.S. health care system. On December 3, 2008, former Democratic Senate majority leader, Thomas Daschle, Obama's designee as secretary of Health and Human Resources and point person on health care, launched an effort to create political momentum when he held a conference call with 1,000 invited supporters who had expressed interest in health issues, promising it would be the first of many opportunities for Americans to weigh in. In addition, there were online videos, blogs, and e-mail alerts as well as traditional public forums. Thousands of people posted comments on health on Change.gov, the Obama transition Web site, which encouraged bloggers to share their concerns and provide their solutions regarding health care policy.[14]

According to Rasiej, "It will be a lot easier to get the American public to adopt any new health care system if they were a part of the process of crafting it." Simon Rosenberg, president of the center-left think tank NDN, was more expansive: "This is the beginning of the reinvention of what the presidency in the 21st century could be." "This will reinvent the relationship of the president to the American people in a way we probably haven't seen since FDR's use of radio in the 1930s."[15]

Democratic political consultant Joe Trippi took the argument a step further, observing that "Obama will be more directly connected to millions of Americans than any president who has come before him, and he will be able to communicate directly to people using the social networking and Web-based tools such as YouTube that his campaign mastered." "Obama's could become the most powerful presidency that we have ever seen," he declared.[16] Republican strategist and the head of White House political operations under Ronald Reagan, Ed Rollins, agreed. "No one's ever had these kinds of resources. This would be the greatest political organization ever put together, *if it works*"[17] (italics added).

That, indeed, is the question. To begin, Obama's team found it difficult to adapt its technologically advanced presidential campaign to government. WhiteHouse.gov was to be the primary vehicle for President Obama to communicate with the masses online. Yet the White House lacks the technology to send mass e-mail updates on presidential initiatives or text messages. The same is true for text messaging, another campaign staple. The White House also has to navigate security and privacy rules regarding the collection of cell phone numbers.[18] In addition, there are time-consuming legal strictures such as a requirement in the Presidential Records Act to archive Web pages whenever they are modified, in order to preserve administration communications. Moreover, the White House cannot engage in overt politicking or fundraising on a government Web site.

The OFA team held several dry runs to test the efficacy of their volunteer apparatus, including a call for supporters to hold "economic recovery house meetings" in February to highlight challenges presented by the recession. The house parties were designed to coincide with the congressional debate over Obama's stimulus package and had mixed results. Although the Obama team touted the 30,000 responses the e-mail drew from the volunteer community and the more than 3,000 house parties thrown in support of the stimulus package, a report in McClatchy Newspapers indicated that several events were sparsely attended.[19]

The first major engagement of OFA in the legislative process began on March 16. An e-mail asked volunteers to go door-to-door on March 21, urging their neighbors to sign a pledge in support of Obama's budget plan. A follow-up message to the mailing list a few days later asked volunteers to call the Hill. A new online tool on the Democratic National Committee's DNC/OFA Web site aided constituents in finding their congressional representatives' contact information so they could call the lawmakers' offices to voice approval of the proposal.

The OFA reported its door-to-door canvass netted about 100,000 pledge signatures while another 114,000 signatures came in through its e-mail network. Republicans scoffed at the effort, arguing that it showed that even most diehard Obama supporters were uncertain about the wisdom of the president's budget plan. Several GOP aides noted that the number of pledges gathered online amounted to fewer than one percent of the names on Obama's vaunted e-mail list. The *Washington Post* reported that interviews with congressional aides from both parties found the signatures swayed few, if any, members of Congress.[20]

By June, OFA was the DNC's largest department, with paid staff members in 31 states and control of the heavily trafficked campaign Web site. Public discourse on health care reform was focusing on the high costs and uncertain results of various proposals, and the White House knew it had to regain momentum. Thus, the president e-mailed millions of campaign supporters, asking for donations to help in the White House's largest-ever issues campaign and for "a coast-to-coast operation ready to knock on doors, deploy volunteers, get out the facts," and show Congress that people wanted change. The DNC deployed dozens of staff members and hundreds of volunteers to 31 states to gather personal stories and build support.[21]

In late-June, it reported roughly 750,000 people had signed a pledge in support of the president's core principles of reducing cost, ensuring quality, and providing choice, including a public insurance option; 500,000 volunteered to help; and several hundred thousand provided their own story for the campaign's use. OFA posted thousands of personal stories online to humanize the debate and overcome criticism of the president's plan. It also trained hundreds of summer volunteers and released its first Internet advertisement—a Virginia man explaining that he lost his insurance when he lost his job.[22]

Nevertheless, the grassroots were not very responsive to the president's call to action. Indeed, his supporters were out-hustled by protests organized by a loose-knit coalition of conservative voters and advocacy groups at meetings held by congressional Democrats and administration officials to discuss health care. The conservative groups, including FreedomWorks, Americans for Prosperity, Right Principles, and Americans for Limited Government, harnessed social networking Web sites to organize their supporters to flood events and heckle and generally disrupt discussion.[23]

PREACHING TO THE CHOIR

When the Obama White House texts its supporters, it is preaching to the choir. There is nothing wrong with that. Perhaps the first rule in the politics of coalition-building is solidifying the base. Yet, the base can only take you so far. Obama received about 53 percent of the national vote, and some of that support was certainly a negative response to George W. Bush in general, and bad economic times in particular. It would be an exaggeration to conclude that Obama's base includes even half the public.

Moreover, widespread home broadband and mobile access to the Internet has created the potential for people to communicate easily with each other as well as to receive communications from leaders. Conservatives have exploited this technology to reinforce their opposition of the new administration. Equally important, however, is the potential for liberals to use the new technologies to oppose the president's evident pragmatism and tendencies toward moderation.

Communications technology users glory in the freedom to dissent that is at the heart of blogging. Even during the transition, there were hints of conflict within the base. Candidate Obama allowed his supporters to wage an online revolt—on his own MyBarackObama.com Web site—over his vote in favor of legislation granting legal immunity to telecommunications firms that participated in the Bush administration's domestic wiretapping program. President-elect Obama, however, did not provide a forum for comments on his YouTube radio address, prompting grumbling among some in the netroots crowd that YouTube without comments was no different from radio.[24]

Internet users are creative, however. The day after Obama announced that the Reverend Rick Warren would deliver the opening prayer at his inauguration, a discussion forum focused on community service instead filled with pages of comments from people opposing the choice. In early January, visitors to Change.gov, the transition Web site, voted a question about whether Obama would appoint a special prosecutor to investigate possible Bush administration war crimes to the top of the questions submitted to the new administration. Progressive Web sites blasted the new administration's efforts to dodge the issue. Within a day, MSNBC's Keith Olbermann picked up the story. A day later, Obama was compelled to answer the question in a TV interview with ABC's George Stephanopoulos, who quoted it and pressed Obama with two follow-ups. Obama's answer, which prioritized moving "forward" but did not rule out a special prosecutor, made the front page of the January 12 issue of the *New York Times*.

The Obama campaign team combined tight top–down message control and campaign coordination with a fair degree of openness at the bottom to independent initiatives by volunteers. As long as everyone agreed on the same underlying goal (beating the Republicans), this approach worked. As that imperative recedes, however, people are going to start pursuing their own objectives, and the architecture that the Obama people have constructed provides them with plenty of opportunities to do so. In March 2009, for example, 63 percent of Republicans but only 49 percent of Democrats approved of Obama's decision to send 17,000 more troops to Afghanistan.[25] This relationship bears watching to see who is setting whose agenda.

The biggest challenge for Obama, however, is winning the hearts and minds of those who are not inclined to support him.

CONVERTING NONSUPPORTERS

The Obama administration began boldly taking its case to the public. Even during the transition, the then president-elect began a full-scale marketing blitz to pass his massive stimulus package, including delivering a major speech at George Mason University. What are the prospects of persuading those who have not favored liberal policies to support the president's proposals? There is nothing in the historical record to suggest success in this endeavor.

In earlier work, I focused on the opinion leadership of Bill Clinton and Ronald Reagan on a wide range of policies and efforts to defend themselves against scandal and found that public opinion rarely moved in the president's direction. On most of Clinton and Reagan's policy initiatives, pluralities— and often majorities—of the public *opposed* the president. Moreover, movement in public opinion was typically *against* the president.[26] An examination of Franklin D. Roosevelt's efforts to lead the public also found the president typically experienced frustration and failure.[27] Similarly, George W. Bush was aggressive in attempting to obtain public support. He, too, typically met with failure.[28]

A CONTEXT OF POLARIZATION

Over his tenure, Barack Obama is likely to be as frustrated at moving public opinion as were his predecessors. To begin, the Obama administration is governing in a context of extreme polarization. We can start with the election results to better understand this context.

Political analyst Jay Cost calculated both unweighted and weighted (where each state is factored according to its share of the nationwide popular vote) averages of Obama's share of the vote in each state plus the District of Columbia to calculate the standard deviation of votes (the greater the standard deviation, the more the states varied around the average, the more accentuated were their differences, and so the more polarization there was). He found the highest level of partisan polarization in the past 60 years. Similarly, if we look at the states that deviated from Obama's share of the nationwide vote (about 52.9 percent) by 10 percentage points or more, we find that there were more "polarized" states than in any election in the past 60 years.[29]

A few states—Vermont, Rhode Island, Hawaii, and the District of Columbia— were polarized in favor of Obama. Most of the polarized states, however, voted for Republican John McCain. The majority of these states form a belt stretching from West Virginia, Kentucky, and Tennessee through Alabama, Mississippi, Louisiana, and Arkansas over to Oklahoma, Kansas, and Nebraska. In addition, Wyoming, Idaho, Utah, and Alaska were strongly in the Republican camp. Many of these states have never before voted so heavily against a victorious Democrat.

The electoral polarization of the Bush years persisted in the 2008 presidential election, indicating that it represents more than a reaction to George W. Bush (although he certainly exacerbated it).[30] The crucial point, however, is that Obama has his work cut out for him to reach the public in states that are turning increasingly red.

Polarization of the electorate has increasingly taken place along economic or class lines. Partisans are more likely to apply ideological labels to themselves and a declining number of them call themselves moderate. Strong party identifiers are the most likely to define politics in ideological terms while the differences in the ideological self-placements of Republicans and Democrats have grown dramatically since the 1980s. This polarization of partisans has contributed to much more ideological voting behavior.[31]

In addition, people now live in communities where their neighbors are likely to agree with them politically and share the same tastes.[32] Nearly half of the 2008 presidential vote came from counties that either Obama or McCain won by 20 percentage points or more. Education levels reinforce this partisan polarization. Among the 96 percent of voters who graduated from high school, Obama did best (58 percent) among those with postgraduate degrees.[33] Homogeneous communities make it even more difficult for the president to change people's views. When Obama's supporters seek support for him, they are likely to be asking those who already agree with them.

EARLY RESISTANCE

As a result of the climate of public opinion and the obstacles to changing opinions, we should not expect Barack Obama, no matter how eloquent his rhetoric, to enjoy substantial long-term success in moving the public in his direction. It is interesting that in the midst of high approval for his perform- ance during the transition, the president-elect met resistance. When he sought the release of the second half of the financial bailout funds—the Troubled Asset Relief Program (TARP)—the average American was not deferring to Obama. Given three choices of what to do with the remaining funds, 62 percent said Congress should block the release unless more details were provided about how the funds would be spent, and another 12 percent replied that Congress should block the funds entirely. Only 20 percent favored Congress's simply allowing the release of the funds.[34]

Things got no better once the president took office. On January 27, the day before the House voted on his stimulus plan, in the midst of a historic economic crisis, after an extensive public relations effort by the White House, and in the glow of the presidential honeymoon, the Gallup poll found that only 52 percent of the public favored Congress passing the stimulus bill. While 73 percent of Democrats favored passage, less than half of the rest of the country agreed—only 46 percent of independents and 29 percent of Republicans.[35] Moreover, public opinion on the stimulus bill was virtually identical to where it stood three weeks before.[36] The public had not moved in the president's direction. A week later, the public still had not moved.[37]

The CBS News/*New York Times* Poll also found that support for the stimulus bill dropped between mid-January and early February, where it stood at just 51 percent.[38] Similarly, Rasmussen Reports polls of likely voters found that on January 19–20, public support stood at 45 percent, which fell to 42 percent by January 27–28, and then down to 37 percent on February 2–3. Unlike the Gallup and CBS/*New York Times* polls, the Rasmussen questions specifically mentioned the bill as being proposed by Barack Obama as well as Democrats in Congress.

At the end of January, Gallup asked whether people supported the presi- dent's stimulus plan as Obama proposed it, wanted "major changes," or want- ed Congress to reject it altogether. Only 38 percent of the public supported passing Obama's stimulus plan as he proposed it, while 37 percent wanted "major changes" and another 17 percent wanted to reject it altogether. Interestingly, only 59 percent of Democrats supported passage of the plan as Obama proposed it, joined by only 37 percent of independents and 13 percent of Republicans. Forty percent of independents wanted major changes.[39]

Near the end of Congress's consideration of the bill, Pew asked the public about "the economic stimulus plan being proposed by the president." It found that 51 percent of those who had heard about the plan said it was a good idea, while 34 percent said it was a bad idea. This support was down from a 57 to a 22 percent ratio in January. Interestingly, support for the proposal was much lower in February than it was in January among those who had "heard a lot" about the economic stimulus. (In February, 46 percent of Americans said they had heard a lot about Obama's stimulus plan). By 49 percent to 41 percent, those who had heard a lot about the proposal saw it as a good idea in February; in January, those who had heard a lot favored it by more than two-to-one.[40]

The biggest legislative battle in Obama's first year was over health care reform. Despite the president's efforts in speeches, news conferences, town hall-style meetings, and interviews to address the public's misgivings, the public did not respond. Instead, it displayed a lack of support for Obama and what the public perceived as his health care plan. It is true that he did not endorse a specific health care plan from among the many bills working their way through House and Senate committees during the spring and summer of 2009. It is possible that some well-informed Americans might have trouble answering a question about "Obama's plan." Nevertheless, he was actively advocating health care reform in this period. Figure 1 gives us a general sense of Americans' impressions of whatever they believed his plan to be.

Figure 1. Support for Health Care Plan

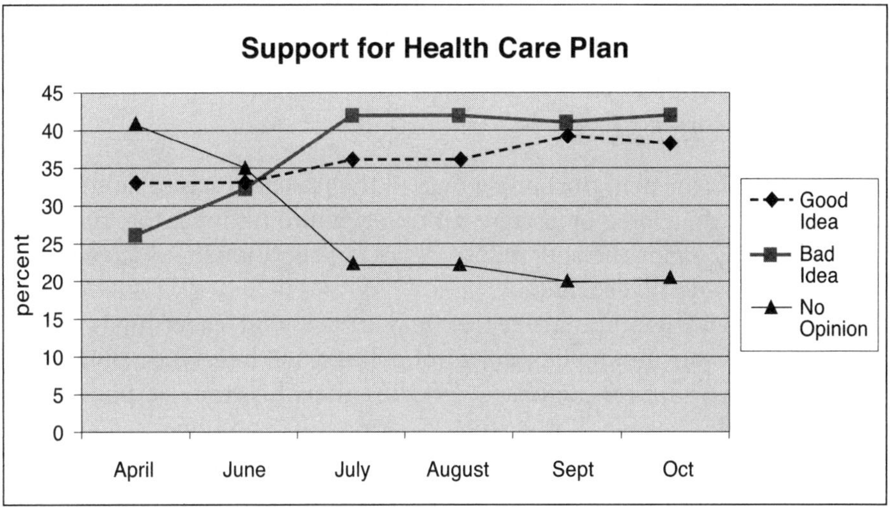

Source: NBC News/*Wall Street Journal* Poll.

Poll Question: "From what you have heard about Barack Obama's health care plan, do you think his plan is a good idea or a bad idea? If you do not have an opinion either way, please say so."

The NBC/*Wall Street Journal* Poll question is especially appropriate for our use because if offered "no opinion" as an option. Opinions were likely to be soft early in the summer because few Americans were closely following the debate on health care until July. June's CBS/*New York Times* Poll, for example, found only 22 percent of Americans saying they have heard or read "a lot" about the health care reform proposals.[41] By late July, the public had become more attentive to the issue. Pew found that health care reform had become the story named most often (31 percent) as the news story Americans said they were following most closely, with 44 percent of the respondents saying they were following it "very closely."[42] In a separate survey, it found that stories about health care filled 25 percent of the newshole.[43]

Two significant trends emerge from the data in Figure 1. First, there was a substantial decrease (19 percentage points) in the percentage of the public with no opinion on the issue between April and July. Second, although support held steady over the period, there was a substantial increase (16 percentage points) in opposition to whatever people perceived to be the Obama's plan. Although we do not have a panel study, it appears that those who formed opinions over the three months from April to July, when debate heated up on health care reform, moved overwhelmingly to opposition. The Pew Research Center similarly found at the end of July that only 38 percent of the public favored the health care proposals Congress was then discussing. Forty-four percent opposed them.[44]

LA PLUS ÇA CHANGE . . .

Some political commentators imply that all the president has to do to obtain the support of the public or Congress is to reach into his inventory of leadership skills and employ the appropriate means of persuasion, but such a view is naive. There is no silver bullet.

It is especially important to recognize that successful leadership is not the result of the dominant chief executive of political folklore, who reshapes the contours of the political landscape and thus alters his strategic position, to pave the way for change. Rather than creating the conditions for important shifts in public policy, such as moving public opinion in their direction, effective leaders are the less-heroic facilitators who work at the margins of coalition-building to recognize and exploit opportunities in their environments. In the long run, president Obama is likely to be no exception.

QUESTIONS TO CONSIDER

1. Why is it so difficult for presidents to influence public opinion?
2. Why is it difficult for the White House to mobilize the president's supporters?
3. What difference is the Internet making in the consideration of major policies like health care reform?

NOTES

[1]Michiko Kakutani, "From Books, New President Found Voice," *New York Times*, January 19, 2009.

[2]Sheryl Gay Stolberg, "A Rewired Bully Pulpit: Big, Bold and Unproven," *New York Times*, November 22, 2008.

[3]Helene Cooper, "On The White House—The Direct Approach," *New York Times*, December 19, 2008.

[4]Stolberg, "A Rewired Bully Pulpit."

[5]Chris Cillizza, "Obama Makes a Point of Speaking of the People, to the People," *Washington Post*, December 14, 2008.

[6]Virginia Heffernan, "The YouTube Presidency—Why the Obama Administration Uploads so Much Video," *New York Times*, April 12, 2009.

[7]People typically turn to the Web sites of traditional news sources for their news, however. See http://blog.nielsen.com/nielsenwire/online_mobile/election-gives-online-news-sites-major-traffic-boost (accessed October 29, 2009).

[8]Pew Research Center for the People & the Press poll, December 3–7, 2008, http://people-press.org; Gallup poll, December 4–7, 2008, http://www.gallup.com. For a broader study, see The Pew Research Center for the People and the Press, *Pew Research Center Biennial News Consumption Survey*, August 2008, http://peoplepress.org/report/444/news-media (accessed October 29, 2009)."]

[9]Michael A. Fletcher and Jose Antonio Vargas, "The White House, Open for Questions," *Washington Post*, March 27, 2009; Sheryl Gay Stolberg, "Obama Makes History in Live Internet Video Chat," *New York Times*, March 27, 2009.

[10]Stolberg, "A Rewired Bully Pulpit."

[11]Pew Internet & American Life Project 2008 Post-Election Survey, November 20–December 4, 2008, http://www.authoring.pewinternet.org/Shared-Content/Data-Sets/2008/November-2008—Post-Election.aspx (accessed October 29, 2009).

[12]Lois Romano, "'08 Campaign Guru Focuses on Grass Roots," *Washington Post*, January 13, 2009.

[13]Peter Wallsten, "Retooling Obama's Campaign Machine for the Long Haul," *Los Angles Times*, January 14, 2009; Associated Press, "Obama Launches Grass-Roots Campaign," January 17, 2009.

[14]Ceci Connolly, "Obama Policymakers Turn to Campaign Tools; Network of Supporters Tapped on Health-Care Issues," *Washington Post*, December 4, 2008.

[15]Ibid.

[16]Cillizza, "Obama Makes a Point."

[17]Wallsten, "Retooling Obama's Campaign Machine for the Long Haul."

[18]Jose Antonio Vargas, "Obama Team Finds It Hard to Adapt Its Web Savvy to Government," *Washington Post*, March 2, 2009.

[19]Chris Cillizza, "Obama Enlists Campaign Army in Budget Fight," *Washington Post*, March 16, 2009.

[20]Dan Eggen, "Obama's Machine Sputters in Effort to Push Budget; Grass-Roots Campaign Has Little Effect," *Washington Post*, April 6, 2009.

[21]Peter Slevin, "Obama Turns to Grass Roots to Push Health Reform," *Washington Post*, June 24, 2009.

[22]Slevin, "Obama Turns to Grass Roots to Push Health Reform."

[23]David M. Herszenhorn and Sheryl Gay Stolberg, "Health Plan Opponents Make Voices Heard," *New York Times*, August 4, 2009.

[24]Stolberg, "A Rewired Bully Pulpit."

[25]Pew Research Center for the People & the Press poll, March 9–12, 2009.

[26]George C. Edwards III, *On Deaf Ears: The Limits of the Bully Pulpit* (New Haven, CT: Yale University Press, 2003).

[27]George C. Edwards III, *The Strategic President: Persuasion and Opportunity in Presidential Leadership* (Princeton, NJ: Princeton University Press, 2009), pp. 26–34.

[28]George C. Edwards III, *Governing by Campaigning: The Politics of the Bush Presidency*, 2nd ed. (New York: Longman, 2007).

[29]Jay Cost, "Electoral Polarization Continues Under Obama," *RealClearPolitics* HorseRaceBlog, November 20, 2008, http://www.realclearpolitics.com/horseraceblog/2008/11/ (accessed October 29, 2009).

[30]See Gary C. Jacobson, *A Divider, Not a Uniter: George W. Bush and the American Public*, 2nd ed. (New York: Longman, 2007).

[31]Nolan McCarty, Keith T. Poole, and Howard Rosenthal, *Polarized America: The Dance of Ideology and Unequal Riches* (Cambridge, MA: MIT Press, 2006).

[32]Bill Bishop, *The Big Sort: Why the Clustering of Like-Minded America Is Tearing Us Apart* (Boston: Houghton Mifflin, 2008).

[33]2000 Exit Polls.

[34]Gallup poll, January 13, 2009.

[35]Gallup poll, January 27, 2009.

[36]Gallup poll, January 6–7, 2009. The question did not specifically mention President Obama.

[37]*USA Today*/Gallup poll, February 4, at http://www.gallup.com.. The question did not specifically mention President Obama.

[38]CBS News/*New York Times* polls of January 11–15, 2009 and February 2–4, 2009.

[39]Gallup poll, January 30–February 1, 2009.

[40]Pew Research Center for the People & the Press poll, February 4–8, 2009.

[41]CBS News/*New York Times* poll, June 12–16, 2009. Fifty percent said they heard or read "some," 23 percent "not much," and 5 percent "nothing."

[42]Pew Research Center for the People & the Press poll, July 24–27, 2009.

[43]Pew Research Center for the People & the Press poll, July 20–26, 2009.

[44]Pew Research Center for the People & the Press poll, July 20–26, 2009.